The Existence of the Mixed Race Damnés

Global Critical Caribbean Thought

Series Editors

Lewis R. Gordon, Professor of Philosophy, UCONN-Storrs, and Honorary Professor, Rhodes University, South Africa

Jane Anna Gordon, Associate Professor of Political Science, UCONN-Storrs

Nelson Maldonado-Torres, Associate Professor of Latino and Caribbean Studies, Rutgers, School of Arts and Sciences

This series, published in partnership with the Caribbean Philosophical Association, turns the lens on the unfolding nature and potential future shape of the globe by taking concepts and ideas that while originating out of very specific contexts share features that lend them transnational utility. Works in the series engage with figures including Frantz Fanon, CLR James, Paulo Freire, Aime Cesaire, Edouard Glissant, and Walter Rodney, and concepts such as coloniality, creolization, decoloniality, double consciousness, and la facultdad.

Titles in the Series

Race, Rights and Rebels: Alternatives to Human Rights and Development from the Global South by Julia Suárez Krabbe
Decolonizing Democracy: Power in a Solid State by Ricardo Sanin-Restrepo
The Desiring Modes of Being Black: Literature and Critical Theory by Jean-Paul Rocchi
Geopolitics and Decolonization: Perspectives from the Global South edited by Lewis R. Gordon and Fernanda Bragato
The Existence of the Mixed Race Damnés: Decolonialism, Class, Gender, Race by Daphne V. Taylor-García

The Existence of the Mixed Race Damnés

Decolonialism, Class, Gender, Race

Daphne V. Taylor-García

London • New York

Published by Rowman & Littlefield International Ltd
Unit A, Whitacre Mews, 26-34 Stannary Street, London SE11 4AB
www.rowmaninternational.com

Rowman & Littlefield International Ltd. is an affiliate of Rowman & Littlefield
4501 Forbes Boulevard, Suite 200, Lanham, Maryland 20706, USA
With additional offices in Boulder, New York, Toronto (Canada), and Plymouth (UK)
www.rowman.com

British Library Cataloguing in Publication Data
A catalogue record for this book is available from the British Library

ISBN: HB 978-1-7866-0615-0

Library of Congress Cataloging-in-Publication Data

Names: Taylor-García, Daphne V., 1973- author.
Title: The existence of the mixed race damnés : decolonialism, class, gender, race / Daphne V. Taylor-García.
Description: New York : Rowman & Littlefield International, 2018. | Series: Global critical Caribbean thought | Includes bibliographical references and index. | Description based on print version record and CIP data provided by publisher; resource not viewed.
Identifiers: LCCN 2018007824 (print) | LCCN 2018022963 (ebook) | ISBN 9781786606167 (electronic) | ISBN 9781786606150 (cloth : alk. paper)
Subjects: LCSH: Racially-mixed people—America—Race identity. | Racially-mixed people—America—Social conditions. | Social classes—America.
Classification: LCC HT1523 (ebook) | LCC HT1523 .T39 2018 (print) | DDC 305.8—dc23
LC record available at https://lccn.loc.gov/2018007824

∞™ The paper used in this publication meets the minimum requirements of American National Standard for Information Sciences—Permanence of Paper for Printed Library Materials, ANSI/NISO Z39.48-1992.

Printed in the United States of America

Contents

Acknowledgments

It is a heartfelt pleasure to write these acknowledgments to the people who have shaped and influenced my intellectual life. I have been extremely fortunate to meet many brilliant and generous people and am deeply appreciative for each one of them.

First, I want to thank Nelson Maldonado-Torres for introducing me to decolonial philosophy and providing me with invaluable training. I am indebted to the scholars who work in this area and consider myself lucky to have attended UC Berkeley when I did. Warm thanks to Laura Elisa Perez for pushing me through that final year of my dissertation. Some of my best memories of UCB are the classes I took with her on queer of color feminisms. I am also grateful to have had the opportunity to work with José Rabasa of the Literature Department. They all profoundly shaped and influenced my intellectual life during my graduate training. Much love and thanks to Chela Sandoval at UC Santa Barbara for being a supportive and inspirational postdoctoral mentor. I learned how to better navigate academia from my time there, and I consider myself very fortunate for that opportunity. My time at UCSB was a rejuvenating one, and for that I'd like to thank the 2005–2010 faculty, postdoctoral fellows, and graduate students of the Chicana/o Studies, Black Studies, and Feminist Studies Departments. I made some lasting friendships with some of the scholars there and want to thank Emily Cheng in particular for always being a supportive listening ear for debriefing on the workings of academia.

My intellectual project can be traced in definitive ways to the Decolonial Feminist working group that we formed as graduate students, and the group continues to flourish in different ways. Thank you in particular to Dalida Maria Benfield, Annie Isabel Fukushima, Yomaira Figueroa, and Xhercis Mendez for our ongoing conversations. Many thanks to George

Ciccariello-Maher for the collaborations we worked on in the Bay Area. My deepest appreciation goes to Roberto Hernandez for his support, integrity, and friendship, as well as for being an intellectual comrade.

Much love to the women of WAVES: Ixayanne Baez, Carmen Johnston, Rosy Fox, and Claudia von Vacano. Our writing sessions sustained me through graduate school and I cherish our lasting friendships. Deepest thanks to Roxanne Dunbar-Ortiz for the support and conversations, and for modeling for me a lifetime of engaged scholar-activism.

I am very lucky to have worked in the Ethnic Studies Department at UC San Diego during the writing of this book alongside Roberto Alvarez, Patrick Anderson, Kirstie Dorr, Fatima El-Tayeb, Yen Le Espiritu, Ross Frank, Dayo Gore, Mattie Harper, Jillian Hernandez, Adria Imada, Sara Kaplan, Roshanak Kheshti, Curtis Marez, Gabriel Mendes, Shelley Streeby, Kamala Visweswaren, Kalindi Vora, and K. Wayne Yang. Special thanks to Boatema Boateng for the friendship and support; to Vanesa Ribas for bringing laughter to the social sciences building; and to Gerardo Arellano for the comradery and collaborations.

Loving gratitude to Fofie Amina Bashir, Maricar Camaya, Antoinette Gonzalez, and Veronica Williams. Through our discussions, collaborations, events, and friendships in San Diego I developed a deeper conviction of what queering people of color spaces consists of and entails. The last chapter in this book is inspired in many ways by the work we did. Thanks too to Fanny Garvey for the fiery conversations. Deepest thanks to Veronica Williams for her support and care; our dinners, walks, and shared laughter sustained me through the writing of this book.

The graduate students of the UCSD Ethnic Studies program are all inspiring scholars. I give special thanks to Jennifer Mogannam for copyediting the reference sections of this book and for collecting the image permissions. I have also had the fortune of working with Mohamed Abumaye, Maria Celleri, Banah Ghadbian, Christina Green, Melissa Linton-Villafranco, Boke Saisi, Seth San Juan, Hina Shaikh, Katherine Steelman, June Yuen Ting, Cynthia Vasquez, Claudia Vizcarra, and Salvador Zarate. The honors undergraduate program in Ethnic Studies and Critical Gender Studies, and the SPACES program all are especially vibrant and I have been fortunate to work with many brilliant students in them, including Eliseo Santos Rivas, Kaneali'I Williams, Mar Velez, Gabby Herencia, Lizzy Gomez, Adriana Rodriguez, Cella Chung, Thomas Ryu Thao, Brendan Francis Alexander-Healy, Noah Olamide, Melanie Leon, Jazzmine Reyes, Mayra Sandoval, Tarangini Saxena, Bianca Harlow, Jaclyn Cerna, Elzbeth Islas, Jessica Hattrick, Nikaria Dixon, and Neil Justin Bascos.

I am extremely grateful for the supportive space of the Caribbean Philosophical Association, particularly the intellectual and organizing work of

Lewis Gordon and Linda Martín Alcoff. Many thanks to Jennifer Lisa Vest for her feedback and encouragement, and I want to give special thanks to Michael Monahan for providing indispensible feedback towards the completion of this book. I also want to thank Ramon Grosfoguel for his support through the Decolonial Summer School in Barcelona.

I am very fortunate to have attended Contact Alternative Secondary School as a youth, the school that is mentioned in this book, and am grateful for the teachers and staff who provided us with the intellectual rigor and committed support that we needed as students. Love to Jenny Blackbird who I have known since those days and our paths have remained intertwined.

My heartfelt thanks goes to my family, both the Garcia-Rios and Pawan-Taylor clans, but especially to my mother, Maria Luisa Taylor; my brother, Chris Taylor, and sister-in-law, Monique Diabo, and their three beautiful children, Stryder, Maria Luisa, and Miguel. I love you all dearly and thank you for your unflinching support.

Introduction

In Frantz Fanon's study of the colonial condition in *Black Skin, White Masks*, it is clear that he is writing against a skepticism that renders the black experience unintelligible. He knows, in fact, that many people reading his book will deny that a black reality exists at all. And yet he writes anyway, insisting that what he says is true. Fanon's turn to the lived experience as a way to elucidate the limits of Eurocentric theories of universalism beseeches all of us to examine our own lived experiences of race, gender, sexuality, and class. It is in this spirit that this book focuses on another experience of nonbeing produced in the antiblack colonial world in which we live: the Afro-Indigenous so-called mixed race experience.

In a semiautobiographical chapter titled, "Being and Not Being, Knowing and Not Knowing," philosopher Jennifer Lisa Vest asks the puzzling question, "Does the mixed person exist?"[1] The contribution is in an edited volume on the mixed race experience where there are numerous articles detailing the situation and, so, it would appear that in a general way mixed race people do indeed exist and there are multiple examples of such a reality. But Vest's query is premised on a particularly Fanonian definition of existence: to exist is to be received in a circuit of reciprocal recognition between individuals. To be is to be able to offer of oneself and have those gifts received. It is the negation of this fundamental and necessary human relationship that animates Fanon's critique. For Vest, however, the condition of a negated intersubjectivity takes a slightly different emphasis from Fanon in that it is not just between colonized and colonizer, but also *between* the colonized. In the "mixed race" schema, a common response is to try to overcome this negation by asserting a singular racial identity and through that move establish the conditions for reciprocal recognition. It is posed as taking a position of difference in unity toward collective strength, but at the expense of often foreclosing a struggle based on the reality of people's actual experiences. The lapse between reality and political identity claims is a rich terrain that, when examined, can provide important insights for elucidating needed analyses to affect social change. Vest responds to this disconnect between reality and contemporary politics with this argument: *existence precedes identity*. It is a phenomenology of the lived experience that Vest is interested in rather than the preemptive assertions of identity claims.

What motivates the emphasis on existence is to unsettle the endemic manifestations of naturalism that tend to pervade race and gender politics, what has been called the politics of purity.[2] The politics of purity is a logic regarding the politics of race that a person can only be of one category and not another with far reaching consequences. This logic is not only specific to the racial categories articulated by Carl Linneaus and Georges-Louis Leclerc, Comte de Buffon, but also to "multiracial" ones, such as *mestiza*, *creole*, *dougla*, and so forth. For example, if one is *mestiza*, then one is not an indigenous tribal member *and* Spanish, respectively, but something new, separate, and different. Similarly, if one is a tribal member in the United States and white passing, the person is a tribal member and not white, and so forth. Similar discussions can be had of identifying as black and indigenous: either one is or is not black and identifying otherwise is sometimes seen as inherently antiblack. Nevertheless, describing the "mixed race" experience can and has been interpreted as undermining indigenous sovereignty and black liberation and/or as obscuring the colonial/racial stratification.[3] Positions such as these on the question of race have been attributed to anticolonial and/or antiracist politics.[4] However, philosophers such as Michael Monahan move in a different direction, raising deep concerns that pervading contemporary race studies scholarship and connected activism is an understanding of race in naturalist terms: that race is real only in so far as it exists as mind-independent properties that are static. One either is or is not a member of a racial group and membership is asserted as a state of being rather than a process of becoming based on individual and collective actions within structural constraints. As a result, even the politics of racial justice, from its naive realist (universal raceless humanity) to its eliminationist (Ignatiev, Roediger) manifestations, successfully present race as fixed categories rather than the situated experiences and decisions of becoming that they are.[5] Rather than try to establish an either/or argument for the racial identity of Afro-indigenous-Asian-European peoples in this book, the terms in which "being mixed" became possible are examined and an argument for a decolonial politics that centers the human as a relationship and as situated becoming is set forth.

AMBIGUITY, CONTENTION, CONTESTATION, AND CONTRADICTION

This book does not seek to assert mixed race as a fixed identity nor as a solution to racial injustice that naively argues "we will all be brown one day and racism will end." Rather working from the premise that antiblackness is the negation of the self/other relationship emergent from the colonization of the Americas that has been epidermalized, this book seeks to illuminate the ways in which some varieties of lived experience were and are characterized as "mixed" in a colonial context and what this reveals to us about racial ontologies, consciousness, and social justice. To this end, this book attends to the historical processes and semiotic structures that made "mixed" subjects possible in an antiblack/colonial world (a fundamentally antihuman world).

The mixed race experience highlights a crucial point that is important for this project. There are two levels on which we can understand the existence of mixed race people: the serial and the group. The *serial* and the *group* are concepts developed by Jean-Paul Sartre, Iris Marion Young, and Sonia Kruks in their examination of social relations.[6] In short, the serial is an ensemble of people who are together oriented toward a particular object but stand in a "plurality of isolations" from one another. An example we can use is to think of a gathering of people standing at the front of a church in colonial Mexico City. This ensemble of people, even if widely varied by age, language, ethnicity, and individual history, are all attuned to the relationship between their individual isolation, of their potential for reciprocity, and of being unified though not necessarily integrated by the colonial project.[7] They do not necessarily talk to each other, and may simply sit or stand waiting for the doors to open. The person's attunement towards this gathering as a group is secondary to their attunement to the family they have not seen in days, the community they have been torn from, what will be expected of them once the doors are opened, what they will say or do, and so forth. Despite their isolation and perhaps even indifference to each other, they share a common interest, and, importantly, they know they exist as a finite and indeterminate plurality of which they are a part. The potential for reciprocity between them is a constant, but it is not predetermined. An identity as a group will emerge only when the common interest is made manifest and when the plurality of isolations is defined as just in relationship to that shared interest. In this example, an external event that might make the group's shared interest evident is when another group of people walk up to the front of the church, open the doors, walk through, and make sure to close the doors—and the waiting people—behind them. The individuals may feel their sense of a shared interest sharpened as their focus turns towards being refused entry to the church. They, as a group, may decide to knock on the door and ask if they can go in, or knock down the doors and take the church as their own, or hold ceremony outside on the front steps. Or the series may be shifted towards a group through talking to one another as best as they can, identifying translators so they can communicate with each more effectively, and evaluating what they have in common that differs from the others that just let themselves into the church. Seriality is thus different from what Sartre defines as a group. A group in fusion is what can develop from a series, but they are not interchangeable nor conflatable. From here, if the experience of refusal continues, they might form into an institutionalized group with meetings, agendas, membership lists, and so forth, that organizes collectively. Or they might dissolve back into seriality. The processual relationship between serials and groups is important to understand as distinct so as to clarify debates on why *describing* one's experience as "mixed race" is not automatically a liberal individualist position, does not presume a particular racial consciousness, and why discussing the phenomenon of being mixed race does not inherently signal a refusal to identify with one or more other groups. The serial is an identifiable ensemble that has not galvanized into a group to take action. Fusing together as a group toward effecting social change is a matter of consciousness, decision making, and the material conditions of possibility that people must navigate. Even as a group, there is no *inherent* characteristic to a group of so-called mixed race people that equates antiblack or anti-indigenous positions. The politics of a group needs to be assessed on the same basis as any political group: on the basis of their actions.

Who exactly is mixed race? Isn't everyone, to some extent? And yet, there is something in the variety of lived experiences that we can and do more readily identify as mixed race from those who are not. This is possible despite the fact that even within this variety of being mixed race, there is a great diversity of experiences, biographies, histories, geographies, and so forth. Identifying someone or a group of people as mixed race often has to do with visibility.[8] As philosopher Linda Martin-Alcoff has demonstrated, when what is visible on the body is understood as truth, there is an interdependence and power relation between what is seen with what is hidden.[9] This interdependence is highlighted in the experience of embodiment of the colonial/racial subject, where what one knows about oneself (such as lineage, family, accomplishments, expertise, intent, history) is superseded by what is visible within the semiotics of the colonial context. This relationship between the visible, embodiment, and social violence was central to Fanon's project and is a growing focus in Latinx Studies.[10] It was a theme raised in *This Bridge Called My Back* and has received spotted systematic attention in Latinx studies since then.[11] Gloria Anzaldua's published essay titled "La Prieta," (the dark-skinned, feminine) and Cherrie Moraga's "La Güera" (the light-skinned, feminine) are included in *Bridge—prieta* and *güera* being two terms used in a commonplace classification of appearance that persists to this day in Latinx communities. Moraga states, "No one ever told me this (that light was right), but I knew that being light was something valued in my family"; Anzaldua begins her essay with memories of being told "Don't go out in the sun. . . . If you get any darker they'll mistake you for an Indian."[12] Anzaldua, "la prieta," tells us it has taken her two years to finish the essay because "each image a sword that cuts through me, each word a test." Both writers point to the linking of human worth and status with morphology and the enormous difficulty in writing about their embodied experience given the ways in which visible race has undercut their kinship ties. Both narratives invoke the scope of material consequences and structural inequalities that are stratified along the color line, a project that this book builds on. The term "colorism" I use throughout this book is a concept developed by Alice Walker in the essay, "If the Present Looks Like the Past, What Does the Future Look Like?" In this piece, Walker focuses on the power relations between black women in the United States in terms of visible race, and I argue that those power relations are relevant and operative across colonial/racial subjects throughout the Americas.[13]

I focus on the Afro-Indigenous mixed race experience with an eye toward the Afro-Indigenous-Asian-European experience because of their significance in the colonization of the Americas and because they exceed the classification schemas of any region or time period. There are no facile groups in which someone of these mixtures can be identified or self-identify without emphasizing one aspect over another. It is a phenomenon of "mixedness" that emerges most particularly in the Caribbean and Latin America, however mixed race people are identified as such all over the world. Colonialism (of multiple types) and coloniality are central in the social and economic structures of typifying particular individuals as *mixed*, whether in early modern Spanish colonialism or contemporary US military colonization. For the purposes of this book, a focus on the legacy of Spanish colonialism in the development of "mixed" as a type of human being will be examined.

THE DECOLONIAL REDUCTION AND "MIXED RACE WOMEN"

The decolonial reduction, a key theoretical framework used in this book, is a term coined by Nelson Maldonado-Torres to denote a particular approach for interpreting the colonial condition. Specifically, the decolonial reduction is a mode of examining forms of life that are "radically affected by a configuration of power that obeys the logic of the relation between master and slave."[14] It is a way of thinking that gives voice to and prioritizes the insights of the colonized, demonstrating how colonization and the institutionalization of the modern/colonial capitalist system has fundamentally bifurcated the world between the colonized and the colonizers and between black and white, overdetermining how we understand the human. (And, just to be clear, in the theoretical framework developed throughout this book, this does not mean that Indigenous peoples, Asians, and Latinxs are irrelevant to the analysis or only recognized as amorphous non-blacks or honorary whites. Black and white are not inherently conflatable with visible race in this book.) It names the insight that there is phenomenon in the world that cannot be explained except through an analysis of the colonial/racial power relations that sustain our current neoliberal world. Specifically, it is an approach to the study of human relations that introduces coloniality as a fundamental axis of reflection in the analysis of power relations, semiotic structures, and identity formations. The logic of colonial and racialized relations continues to define contemporary social relations despite formal decolonization in many parts of the world such as Latin America and the Caribbean, and significant economic and governmental changes in places such as the United States and Canada. Focusing on the persistent logics of colonialisms gives voice to a conception of time that emphasizes it as a set of social relations that stands in contrast to dominant understandings of time as linear, developmental, and/or radically differentiated across centuries due to policy shifts and/or technological innovations. Coloniality makes evident the sedimentation of racialized and gendered relations despite other aspects of social change.

The theories of coloniality explain how the system of social classification wrought under colonialism in the Americas was more than a question of proletarianization, but also of racialization and gendering.[15] Namely, that the colonization of the Americas not only invented new forms of labor control, but also introduced an ontological shift: new terms for understanding the human that went beyond what a strict analysis of class could explain. Slavery for black Africans, various forms of coerced cash-crop labor (*repartimiento, mita, peonage*) for Native Americans, and indentured labor for the European working class paired groups of ethnicities with certain types of labor and ascribed an ontological hierarchy to these relations that have yet to be fully accounted.[16] An area that requires further examination is the race/labor roles ascribed to *castas*—the natally alienated "mixed" peoples. Thus far, it is understood that the legacy of Spanish (and later British, French, Dutch, and American) colonial/racial ideology situated black Africans as "natural slaves," American Indians as a childlike group that could be raised to full human status through cultural assimilation and miscegenation, and Spaniards/bourgeois Europeans were the only fully-human beings in the colonial scene. This triadic schema was reflected in the colonial division of labor.[17] In this redefinition of the human over the course of three centuries vis-à-vis the exploitation of land and labor in the Spanish viceroyalties and British colonies, a crucial aspect was to impose a gender system that created different arrangements for colonized males and females than it did for European bourgeois colonizers.[18] What is less clear from these foundational texts is how *castas* were positioned in the triadic schema. For example, a careful reading between the lines for gender in Patricia Seed's records on race and the division of labor in Mexico City (Seed includes gender as one of the categories in her summaries of primary documents, but the following is my own analysis) reveals that Spanish women in the capital of the viceroyalty of New Spain very rarely worked outside the home, but when they did it was in the capacity of elite positions such as estate owner or schoolmistress, a socioeconomic status dominated almost exclusively by Spanish peninsular men.[19] The "private" domain of the home was indeed where Spanish women in the colonies were subordinated to Spanish men, but in turn they exerted power over the black, indigenous, and *casta* people who they enslaved or employed. Specifically, the majority of free black men worked as servants in mid-eighteenth-century Mexico City. Indian men worked largely as laborers, but also as servants and artisans (a more prestigious employment position) in significant numbers. Free mulatos worked either as servants or artisans in almost equal numbers. Mestizos worked largely as artisans, but also as servants and laborers in significant numbers. Castizos worked mostly as artisans, but they are also the first *casta* group to start appearing in more significant numbers in elite positions. In other words, we do see a fairly consistent upward trajectory of socioeconomic statuses as ratios of European blood increase among men, with the most prestigious positions, that of shop owners, merchants, and estate owners, reserved for Spanish peninsulars. But if we hone in on the gendered/raced division of labor we see another crucial development: most free black women along with free black men, indigenous women, mulattas, and mestizas labored almost exclusively as servants.[20] The gendered/raced division of colonial labor systems thus raises important questions for decolonial feminism. Gender was not a significant factor on which labor positions were divided between free black men and free black women, but for other colonial/racial subjects, gender is deployed to stratify *casta* and indigenous men from *casta* and indigenous women. Furthermore, not only were new forms of labor control introduced through Spanish colonization along racial lines between black, indigenous, and European, but it also tied race and labor positions to specific *castas*. We will see in this book that this had to do with the colonial mission and intellectual project to assimilate *castas* into a Spanish colonial hierarchy where the division of labor took on new meaning and black peoples were situated as the nadir. Identifying the full scope of the logic of this system, what can be referred to as the coloniality of being, has been the work of decolonial feminism, beginning with questioning what gender means and how it works in a Manichean antiblack and colonial world.[21]

A NOTE TO UNSETTLE AREA STUDIES APPROACHES: ON THE VICEROYALTY OF NEW SPAIN

One of the geopolitical references that are made in chapters 2 and 3 of this book is "the viceroyalty of New Spain." The Viceroyalty of New Spain was an administrative body under the Spanish crown that existed as such for three centuries: 1521–1821. New Spain was the first of four of Spain's viceroyalties, and Mexico City was its capital. This viceroyalty was comprised of a territory that included present-day Mexico, Central America, much of the southwestern and central United States, the Spanish West Indies, Spanish Florida, and the Spanish East Indies. The Spanish West Indies consisted of Cuba, Haiti, the Dominican Republic, Puerto Rico, Saint Martin, the Virgin Islands, Anguilla, Montserrat, Guadalupe and the Lesser Antilles, Jamaica, the Cayman Islands, Trinidad, and the Bay Islands. What I want to underscore here is how the history of New Spain forces a researcher to be mindful of a geography that exceeds the logic of contemporary area studies. Countries that are now considered absolutely distinct, for example the United States, Mexico, and Trinidad, were all part of the Viceroyalty of New Spain. Thus, taking a dominant area studies mind frame to the study of the history of colonization is not helpful and even counter to the effort at hand. While each of these regions named above have distinct cultures, social structures, and histories, they are also imbricated in a shared history of Spanish colonization.[22]

My own family's history is situated in the country of Mexico on the maternal side and Trinidad and Tobago on the paternal side. The effort to understand the historical forces at play in my own genealogy has forced me to jump in and across numerous fields of study, even those that formed as a critique of area studies: Latinx Studies, Caribbean Studies, Chicanx Studies, Black Studies, and Indigenous Studies. What became apparent to me through this intellectual border crossing was that there was a concrete historical context that intertwined these distinct fields and demanded a different way of thinking about regions of study. How is one to think about the history of the present when the Viceroyalty of New Spain is the geographic region of the colonial legacy one is grappling with? Most authors are forced to abandon the historical magnitude of New Spain and focus on one region: the United States, or the Philippines, or the Dominican Republic, and so forth.[23] The implications are far reaching: twentieth-century intellectual work from Trinidad is seen as irrelevant or even wrong to the study of Mexico or the southwestern United States and vice versa, Jamaica and Trinidad are not commonly included in Latinx Studies, and so on. However, for anywhere between 150 to 300 years these disparate regions were tied together under a shared colonial administration. The laws that were passed and practices that were established by

Spanish colonists, both in Spain and in Mexico City, impacted these different regions in different ways, so there is a need for further research on the concrete manifestations of colonial policy across these different regions. Chapter 2 of this book contributes to the study of Mexico City, the capital of the Viceroyalty of New Spain (that may prove to have wider relevance), where slavery was an urban institution (rather than a rural one as in the United States) and the *sistema de castas* was a clearly developed labor and social system. That chapter reveals that the logic of race, gender, and socioeconomic relations that were institutionalized under direct Spanish colonial rule has not yet been undone.

Given that a study of the lifeworld and the semiotic structures that make the lived experience communicable is a central theme in my research, focusing on only one area studies demarcated region was neither possible nor desirable. My own lived experience is constituted by a simultaneously West Indian and Mexican home life in the settler colonial nation-state of Canada and then the United States. In fact, the relevance of the lived experience pushed me to question the terms of readily accepted geographic and cultural configurations, from "Latin America" to "North America," from "Europe" to the "Americas." As a result, chapter 2 discusses the *logic* of racial hierarchies established under Spanish colonial rule broadly speaking, particularly regarding "mixed race" people, and the third chapter focuses on unsettling the naturalization of the construction of continents as racialized designations in the first century of Spain's colonial project. The fourth chapter seeks a way in which to find a decolonial political voice that re-centers the human as a relationship between people who have been systematically dehumanized through these projects.

BEING "MIXED RACE" AND THE PROBLEM OF IDENTIFICATION FOR TAKING ACTION

What if you were born "mixed?" Of red, black, and Asian histories in a white world, but read as visibly ambiguous? How would you call on your people? What term would you use to identify yourself or to galvanize others? The mixed race experience raises some fundamental questions about being in a world where racial identities are always assumed to be visibly either/or. A contemporary example of the challenges that mixed race people encounter in efforts to overcome bad faith can be found in discussions about Hugo Chávez's race. Right after Chávez's sweeping democratic victory in the 2006 Venezuelan elections, social media sites were full of questions about his race. "*What is he*?" littered blog posts. An article published in *Counterpunch* in 2005 was reposted to answer the question: "Physically, Hugo Chávez is a *pardo*, a term used in the colonial period to denote someone of mixed racial roots." Chávez's features, writes another magazine columnist, "are a dark-copper color and as thick as clay; he has protruding, sensuous lips and deep-set eyes under a heavy brow. His hair is black and kinky. He is a burly man of medium height, with a long, hatchet-shaped nose and a massive chin and jaw." Chávez is noted in the article for speaking proudly of his diverse heritage; his grandmother on his father's side was a Pumé Indian, and his grandfather was black. The way in which gender has shaped his life is not mentioned, but the article points out that, like many other mixed race Venezuelans, Chávez grew up in poverty. In these types of descriptions there is a presupposition that colonial racialization is reducible to a continental ontology; a presupposition I push to move away from in this book.

We can consider some of the issues that complicate a transcolonial/transnational legibility of race and categorization in Chavez's example. For instance, out of all the possible census options, which one would someone like Chavez identify as in the United States? The term *pardo* is unintelligible here; he is not considered *black* in Venezuela nor would he likely be in the US. *Hispanic* is a racialized designator, but we are asked to specify whether White, Black, Indigenous, or Asian. It is not clear if Chavez maintains a tribal affiliation or community attachment with his father's maternal side as the US census specifies, and the discourse of tribal citizenship does not easily translate across to the Venezuelan context. *Mestizo*, which some might suggest as an option that is not on the census, has a specific history as a racial designation and is not generally used by people of African ancestry in the United States, nor by most people outside of academia. People argued over whether Chávez was black, brown, or white, and thus, where his political commitments lay. The issue of "being mixed" from Latin America presents a formidable obstacle in US-based social movements where organizing efforts coalesce around a particular history of race and identity. For those who trace their history to an ex-Spanish colony, the question of "mixedness" is often unavoidable and requires speaking to not only Black/White or Indian/White "mixing," but Black/White/Indigenous/Asian "mixing," because it mattered historically and continues to define our sense of self in the contemporary moment. The Pew Research Center has published numerous reports on the conundrum of racial identity and Latinx in the United States.[24] The semiotic structures that make "being mixed" a legible concept was created in the colonial period and the confluence of history, visuality, and action continues to shape different positionalities today. It is the emergence of "mixed" as a way of speaking about human difference that is the focus of chapter 2. The history of "being mixed" raises fundamental questions about the naturalization of not only discrete racial categories that emerged directly from colonial and imperial projects, but the very conceptualization of "mixing" races. It also raises questions for those supposedly born at the interstices of racial differences: under what rubric are we to mobilize in a North American context? This question is pertinent as Latinxs in the United States and Canada grapple with identifying as being Indigenous, Black, White, and/or Asian, and so forth, on census forms and in political affiliations in North America.

STUDYING MIXED RACE EXISTENCE THROUGH AN INTERSECTIONAL LENS

A desire to examine the intersubjectivity of the mixed race experience was a central motivation in writing *The Existence of the Mixed Race Damnés*. On the other hand, it became immediately apparent that the available terms through which I might be expected to describe my own experiences needed to be interrogated. For example, I might have been expected to identify my positionality as *mestiza*, a woman, and as working class, but none of these conventions seemed to adequately define or describe my positionality in the world. If the purpose is to think of new ways of being human, an accurate description of the dehumanized world is helpful. What I have sought to do here instead, is to grapple with the semiotic structures of colonialism that invented the mixed race experience, to develop a term for the colonial/racial working class, and make clear the parameters of gender in a colonial context.

The Existence of the Mixed Race Damnés examines the semiotic structures of coming to an oppositional consciousness as a Spanish colonial subject in a settler-colonial metropole. The book begins from the first-person experience to elucidate the historical-racial structures through which working class mixed race Latinxs are constructed. Rather than naturalize identifications with a particular class, race, or gendered positionality, *The Existence of the Mixed Race Damnés* looks to the constructed nature of experience, how notions of being mixed race and a woman in the colonies were first produced and unsettles the sedimented ways in which the mixed race woman is read as a particular set of signs in the colonial context of continental logics.

The Existence of the Mixed Race Damnés was greatly inspired by the path breaking work of Frantz Fanon, which brought race, gender, sexuality, and class to the forefront of embodied philosophy and foregrounded the lived experience of colonial/racial subjects, historical-racial schemas, the restructuring of the socio-economic world, and knowledge production in the redefinition of the human.

The two organizing questions—From where and in what form does the spirit of resistance arise in a world that mitigates against one's existence? And, who am I in reality in a colonial world?—is inspired by Fanon's examination of the same questions, but with an emphasis on the Spanish colonial mixed race experience and questions of class and gender. Drawing from these problematics, the book leaves "methods to the botanists and mathematicians" and engages a wide variety of approaches to draw out the existential challenges of being a working class "mixed race" woman seeking to overcome bad faith and colonial logic.

THE EXISTENCE OF THE MIXED RACE DAMNÉS: KEY TERMS

Some of the terms that I use in this book have a very particular meaning that may differ significantly from the ways in which the terms are used in everyday language or in much Ethnic Studies scholarship. Rather than provide a dictionary of terms in a standard format, I will use a poem by Jennifer Lisa Vest that captures the spirit of the inquiry and helps explain key concepts and terms.

The histories of slavery and colonialisms provide us with multiple examples of creating "new worlds" in the direst of conditions, and yet the agency of the oppressed appears impossible to some. *Demands of Existence* by Vest asks key questions about choosing to go on despite an impossible situation, the ethics of such a choice, and thus succinctly encapsulates the fundamentals of taking action from the underside of modernity.[25] The poem also provides me with the opportunity to explain key terminology that I will be using throughout this book.

If I told you to do the impossible
To fight the impossible fight
To pursue the impossible dream
If I told you it was the only thing that would
Make you possible
Would you do it?

If I colored you black or red and set you down in this white world
If I shaped you woman and set you down in this man's world
If I fashioned you queer and set you down in this straight world
If I told you to do the impossible
To fight the impossible fight
To pursue the impossible dream
If I told you it was the only thing that would
Make you possible
Would you do it?

What are the "demands of existence?" To put it in terms that may make the concept more easily understood: queer women of color, and colonial/racial subjects generally, people of color from the working class live in a world that constantly mitigates against their very existence. Facing death is a daily affair rather than a singular event at the end of a long life, a modern ethos that Julia Suarez-Krabbe has called the death project.[26] In the face of constant premature death, eventually one has to ask, why go on?[27] Choosing to go on, and the decisions that must follow, speaks to the demands of existence. The demands of existence foreground that at a fundamental level we are always in a process of making decisions about the kind of life we want to live within the constraints of the structures in which we live. In fact, in a colonial/antiblack world it becomes apparent that it is only through struggling for a new world that colonial/racial subjects can exist. Conversely, colonial/racial subjects can take another route. They can be confronted with their dehumanized condition and choose to embrace a pleasing falsehood about it, such as "I am not like these other people here," rather than a displeasing truth such as "I am exactly who they are talking about."[28] It is the embracement of pleasing falsehoods that is what fundamentally defines "bad faith" in this book: when we refuse to take responsibility for what we can in fact take responsibility for or the converse, when we assert ourselves as pure transcendence. When Vest asks us, "Would you do it?" she is bringing attention to our choice to say either yes or no and the agency that is involved in confronting one's dehumanization. When audiences respond with a "no" to Vest's question it also highlights the limits of intersubjectivity in a colonial/racial world: the person who is asked to relate to the condition of the damnés but does not come from it, often cannot fathom the damnés' agency. The history of slave rebellions and contemporary organizing for prisoners' rights from the cells of solitary confinement or organizing for healthy communities by residents of public housing projects are not within the "no" frame of reference.

To be put down on this earth and racialized as a person of color, to be identified at birth as male, female, or intersex, to be gendered as a man, woman, queer, and so forth, or to prefer heterosexual relationships or something else in the spectrum of sexual orientations, speaks to our *facticity*. Facticity is the term used to speak to the aspects of our lives that make up our histories and the conditions we have inherited by virtue of where we were born. These histories and conditions range from the languages we speak, the religions we practice, to our citizenship statuses. In addition to the social structures we are born into, our facticity also includes all the decisions we have made in our lives that have brought us to this current moment and connect us to our possible futures.

If I told you your life was absurd
And unfair and that the cards would be stacked
Ridiculously against you
But that you should live nonetheless

That you must live nonetheless
Would you do it?

Our facticity is not only our past but is also the immediate choices we are making and will make as we move through the world. A key aspect of the demands of existence is that we are not automatons that respond without recourse to the circumstances we have inherited, no matter how difficult they may be. We are also conscious beings who make decisions that affect our futures, from how we interpret our pasts to how we respond to our current circumstances. In Vest's poem, she is asking these very types of existential questions: If born to a hellish existence, can you go on? Can you come up with a plan in a situation in which you are threatened with death and try to make the plan a reality? For millions of people around the world, the answer has been *yes*.[29] It is our *consciousness* that provides us with this capacity to respond in various ways to our circumstances and give meaning to our lives. It is in this sense that we are always more than our pasts or the conditions in which we were born. Together, our facticity and consciousness constitute our *situations*, and it is from our situations that our consciousness is oriented toward the world in a particular way.[30]

Now, what if I was to treat my facticity as an inevitable fate, as facts of my life that I could do little about? For example, what if I was shaped a woman of color and put down in a white man's world and I accepted my subjugation as God's plan? What if I was born to an economic situation where employers treated me as dispensable and I accepted their actions toward me as part of the natural world? Or conversely, what if I treated my facticity as irrelevant and asserted myself as pure transcendence, as if my race, gender, and economic position did not matter nor tell me something important about reality? To treat one's life as a ready-made world where one has no choice *or* to consider the structural limits of the world as irrelevant is referred to as *bad faith*. Rather, we are beings constantly negotiating our agency within the structural constraints we face, and these differ across color, gender, class, and so forth. Bad faith is the refusal to accept responsibility, however constrained or limited, of making a judgment and taking an action regarding our circumstances while facing reality.

The circumstances for the damné may be overwhelming, but even in these situations we can think, "I deserve better than this" and try to figure out how to make it happen, rather than, for instance, accept the terms we are handed as part of greater scheme beyond our reproach. Although cynicism, pessimism, and nihilism are possible responses to overwhelming circumstances that people do take, the explanation here underscores that even these latter positions are based on decisions that the individual chooses to make. The question that immediately arises when the scope and depth of the socioeconomic structures that militate against the existence of colonial/racial subjects is realized, is what action do I take? What ethics do I foreground? What relationships do I prioritize?

In Vest's poem she asks, "If your flock was a ragged and desperate band of thieves, your children thugs and your own mother addicted to drugs, would you have the strength to lead them? Would you have the heart to love them? Would you have the humility to call yourself one of them? To claim their faults as your own?" With these questions Vest is asking us to think about how we identify with our people, other poor people of color, by particularly highlighting those involved in stigmatized, alternative economies and may be struggling with mental health issues. These questions Vest asks are not necessarily directed toward those of the upper classes but have to do with the relations *between* the damnés. Do we humble ourselves and act with kindness and generosity toward each other? How do we understand poverty, property-related crimes, criminalization, and drug addiction? The poem implores us to respond with thoughts and acts of love, humility, and collective identification with those of us cast by dominant narratives as "below." To love and be humble with an other is to prioritize the other's well-being. This involves, among other things, communication and being responsive and responsible to the other.[31] The way in which we respond to these questions are part and parcel of the demands of existence. Vest ends with a call to responsible action: "Would you do it?" For it is through our actions that we fashion ourselves and the world around us. Even if we choose to do nothing at all, that is still a choice and speaks to the quotidian ways in which the relationship between the individual and social structures are defined by the actions we take.

Implicit to Vest's poem is an invocation of the self/other relationship. When she asks us to imagine ourselves in the shoes of another person's experience, it highlights the role of mental images in one's understanding of who the other is. In much Ethnic Studies scholarship the other (such as in Edward Said's *Orientalism*) is a term used to refer to an already negatively racialized group. Similarly, "othering" will often mean the process of negatively racializing a group of people. However, this is not the way in which the term "other" is used in this book. In this book the other is used in the way invoked in Vest's poem: the other is any other person with whom I can potentially establish communication. The robust self/other relationship where two people recognize each other as conscious beings with a unique and valuable perspective of the world, is precisely the kind of self/other relationship that is denied in a colonial/racial context.[32] The self/other relationship is, in this book, a norm that the colonized struggle to attain. For a further example of the negation of the self/other relationship in a colonial context, see Trinh Minh Ha's discussion of anthropology in *Native, Woman, Other: Writing Postcoloniality and Feminism* (Bloomington: Indiana University Press, 1989).

A final note on terminology: I chose to use the term "casta" in it's Spanish form instead of translating to "caste" to signal the colonial context in which the category was developed in the Americas. I also use the terminology of "mixed race" instead of only "mestizaje" in this book, in part because the study traverses US, Canadian, and Mexican racial constructions with an eye toward contributing to a critical discussion of race and Latinidad. I also use "mixed race" to encourage a dialogue between the multitude of peoples around the world impacted by the designation of mixed race. Even though the mixed race experience is often thought to be entirely unique to a given region, through my research on this topic, I have come to the conclusion that the logic of mixed race designations follows a similar pattern of coloniality, notions of a racial hierarchy and purity, and continental ontologies, even as they are uniquely adapted to the conditions at hand.

NOTES

1. Jennifer Lisa Vest, "Being and Not Being, Knowing and Not Knowing," in *Philosophy and the Mixed Race Experience*, ed. Tina Fernandes-Botts (Lanham, MD: Rowman & Littlefield, 2017), 93–116.

2. Michael Monahan, *The Creolizing Subject* (New York: Fordham University Press, 2011), 119.

3. Chris Anderson, *Metis: Race, Recognition, and the Struggle for Indigenous Peoplehood* (Vancouver: UBC Press, 2014); Jared Sexton, *Amalgamation Schemes* (Minneapolis: University of Minnesota Press, 2008).

4. Monahan, *The Creolizing Subject*, 19–50.

5. Ibid., 72.

6. Jean-Paul Sartre, *Critique of Dialectical Reason, Volume 1*, trans. Alan Sheridan-Smith (London: New Left Books, 1960); Iris Marion Young, "Gender as Seriality: Thinking about Women as a Social Collective," *Signs* 19, no. 3 (Spring 1994): 713–38; Sonia Kruks, "Identity Politics and Dialectical Reason: Beyond an Epistemology of Provenance," *Hypatia* 10, no. 2 (Spring 1995): 1–22.

7. Jean-Paul Sartre, *Critique of Dialectical Reason, Volume 1,* trans. Alan Sheridan-Smith (London: New Left Books, 1960), 256–269.

8. Linda Martin-Alcoff, *Visible Identities: Race, Gender, and the Self* (New York: Oxford University Press, 2006), 7–8.

9. Ibid.

10. I use the "x" in "Latinx" to signal Maria Lugones' critique of gender across the colonial divide: namely that it does not operate in the same way for colonial/racial subjects.

11. What Eduardo Bonilla-Silva terms "pigmentocracy" is a growing Latinx Studies field examining the way in which colorism stratifies social relations in Latin America, North America, and Europe. Eduardo Bonilla-Silva, "The Latin Americanization of U.S. Race Relations: A New Pigmentocracy," in *Shades of Difference: Why Skin Color Matters*, ed. E. N. Glenn (Palo Alto, CA: Stanford University Press, 2009), 40–60; Edward Tellez, *Pigmentocracies: Ethnicity, Race, and Color in Latin America*

(Chapel Hill: The University of North Carolina Press, 2014); Ian Haney Lopez, *White by Law* (New York: New York University Press, 2006); George Yancy, *Who Is White?: Latinos, Asians, and the New Black/Nonblack Divide* (Boulder, CO: Lynne Rienner Publishers, 2003); Daniel Zizumbo-Colunga and Iván Flores Martínez. "Is Mexico a Post-Racial Country? Inequality and Skin Tone across the Americas," Latin American Public Opinion Project, 2017.

12. Cherrie Moraga, "La Guera," in *This Bridge Called My Back*, ed. Cherrie Moraga and Gloria Anzaldua (Boston: Kitchen Table/Women of Color Press, 1983), 25; Gloria Anzaldua, "La Prieta," in *This Bridge Called My Back*, ed. Cherrie Moraga and Gloria Anzaldua (Boston: Kitchen Table/Women of Color Press, 1983), 220.

13. Alice Walker. "If the Present Looks Like the Past, What Does the Future Look Like?" *In Search of Our Mother's Garden*.

14. Nelson Maldonado-Torres, *Against War: Views from the Underside of Modernity* (Durham, NC: Duke University Press, 2008), 102.

15. For a further discussion of the coloniality of being that is pertinent to this book, see Sylvia Wynter, "1492: A New World View," in *Race, Discourse, and the Origin of the Americas*, ed. Vera Lawrence Hyatt et al. (Washington, DC: Smithsonian Institution Press, 1995); Sylvia Wynter, "Unsettling the Coloniality of Being/Power/Truth/Freedom: Towards the Human, After Man, Its Overrepresentation—An Argument," *CR The New Centennial Review* 3 (2003): 257–333; Nelson Maldonado-Torres, "On the Coloniality of Being: Contributions to the Development of a Concept," *Cultural Studies* 21 (2007): 240; "Post-Continental Philosophy: Its Definition, Contours, and Fundamental Sources," *Worlds and Knowledges Otherwise* 1, no. 3 (2006): accessed July 31, 2016, https://globalstudies.trinity.duke.edu/wp-content/themes/cgsh/materials/WKO/v1d3_NMaldonado-Torres.pdf; Nelson Maldonado-Torres, "The Topology of Being and the Geopolitics of Knowledge," *City: An Analysis of Urban Trends, Culture, Theory, Policy, Action* 8 (March 2004): 29–56; Lugones, "Heterosexualism and the Colonial/Modern Gender System."

16. Anibal Quijano, "The Coloniality of Power, Eurocentrism, and Latin America," *Nepantla: Views from South* 1 (2000): 533–80.

17. See Anthony Pagden, *The Fall of Natural Man* (Cambridge: Cambridge University Press, 1987).

18. Maria Lugones, "Heterosexualism and the Colonial/Modern Gender System," *Hypatia* 22 (Winter 2007): 186–209.

19. This argument is not the one Patricia Seed makes in the article cited below. Rather, I extrapolate this analysis through an examination of the charts she provides that specifies the gender of laborers in addition to their race. Seed focuses on the race and labor aspect, and I further the analysis by highlighting the role of gender in the racialized division of labor. Patricia Seed, "Social Dimensions of Race: Mexico City, 1753," *The Hispanic American Historical Review* 62 (1982): 569–606. This method of rereading established historical narratives to further the decolonial project is explained in Linda Tuhiwai Smith's book *Decolonizing Methodologies*.

20. Ibid.

21. Maria Lugones, "The Coloniality of Gender," *Worlds & Knowledges Otherwise* 2, no. 2 (Spring 2008): 1.

22. Martin W. Lewis and Karen Wigen, *The Myth of Continents: A Critique of Metageography* (Berkeley: University of California Press, 1997), 13–14.

23. An art exhibit curated by Tatiana Flores at the Museum of Latin American Art in 2018, titled "Relational Undercurrents: Contemporary Art of the Caribbean Archipelago," is an excellent example that stands against this tendency.

24. "The Many Dimensions of Hispanic Racial Identify," last modified June 11, 2015, http://www.pewsocialtrends.org/2015/06/11/chapter-7-the-many-dimensions-of-hispanic-racial-identity; "Afro-Latino: A Deeply Rooted Identity among U.S. Hispanics," last modified March 1, 2016, http://www.pewresearch.org/fact-tank/2016/03/01/afro-latino-a-deeply-rooted-identity-among-u-s-hispanics; "Is Being Hispanic a Matter of Race, Ethnicity, or Both?," last modified June 15, 2016, http://www.pewresearch.org/fact-tank/2015/06/15/is-being-hispanic-a-matter-of-race-ethnicity-or-both.

25. "The underside of modernity" or "the dark side of modernity" are terms coined by coloniality theorists to underscore that there is a fundamental, but not often acknowledged, side of modernity: coloniality.

26. Nelson Maldonado-Torres, *Against War* (Durham, NC: Duke University Press, 2008); Achille Mbembe, "Necropolitics," *Public Culture* 15, no. 1 (Winter 2003): 11–40; Julia Suarez-Krabbe, *Race, Rights, Rebels: Alternatives to Human Rights and Development from the Global South* (Lanham, MD: Rowman & Littlefield, 2016), 4.

27. Lewis Gordon, "Race, Theodicy, and the Normative Emancipatory Challenges of Blackness," *South Atlantic Quarterly* 112 (October 2013).

28. Lewis Gordon, *Bad Faith and Antiblack Racism* (Amherst, NY: Humanity Books, 1995), 8.

29. Frantz Fanon, *Black Skin, White Masks* (New York: Grove Press, 2008), 12.

30. Sara Ahmed, *Queer Orientations: Orientations, Objections, Others* (Durham, NC: Duke University Press, 2006).

31. I insert this definition because of the cynicism that surrounds the term "love." The term is often misused and abused leaving many people ambivalent and uninterested in theories that speak of "love." For further discussion of being responsive and responsible to others see Cressida Hayes, "Changing Race, Changing Sex: The Ethics of Self-transformation," *Journal of Social Philosophy* 2, no. 37 (Summer 2006): 266–82.

32. Lewis Gordon, *Existencia Africana: Understanding Africana Existential Thought* (New York: Routledge, 2000), 85.

Chapter 1

Toward a Phenomenology of the Sub-Proletariat

In the metropole, the damné's situation (defined here as the capacity of the damné's consciousness to go beyond the givens of the structures we have inherited) is borne in and through the brick, mortar, and streetlights of the deindustrialized neighborhood called home. Seeing oneself through the eyes of the other in the neoliberal city, housing project residents, welfare recipients, and food program participants take a central role in these reflections. "Being seen" involves the realization that one is not only a subject that faces the world, but also an object in the eyes of the other that desires their recognition. Narratives of low-income public housing, whether in the inner city, *banlieues*, or the suburbs, are the stories of the otherwise-homeless and function as the zero-degree against which other socioeconomic groups define themselves. It is in these places of the modern/colonial city where the damnés' dreams, actions, prophetic imaginations, and yearnings rub raw against the material conditions of the coloniality of capitalism.

Race and gender have received significant attention in phenomenological studies, however, class has been the explicit focus of only two book-length projects.[1] There are several reasons for this in the neoliberal university, all of which overlap with each other. One, the failure of a multiracial working-class consciousness to galvanize in response to late capitalism has led many academics to deride any mention of the existence of class at all, but this has curiously also meant the elision of a substantive phenomenology of socioeconomic divisions. Two, definitions of class are often reduced to current income, and there is little understanding of the political consciousness that is explicit in Marx's definition of class. In other words, class is reduced to liberal individualist terms. Three, the fact that most PhDs of color are from the middle class creates an intellectual culture where substantive analyses of socioeconomic differences among the damnés are left to empiricists to account for a world "out there." Theories of embodiment have, for these reasons, focused on race, gender, and sexuality, but not class. Departing from this tendency, this chapter works toward a phenomenology of racialized and gendered class conditions in a settler colonial metropole.

THE SUB-PROLETARIAT/THE DAMNÉS

The lumpenproletariat, as the derided class category in Marx's works, was the site of crucial reconfiguration in the thought of Mao Tse-tung, Amílcar Cabral, Frantz Fanon, and several members of the Black Panther Party. All saw the importance of economics in the structuring of social relations, but also that the situation for white Europeans was quite different than for people of color. The schema that Marx offered misidentified the revolutionary potential of peasants, did not foresee the processes of urbanization of peasants without industrialization that would characterize colonial capitals, and did not explain that the relationship between the proletariat and the lumpenproletariat was always in flux: the working class could become "the lumpen" at any time and vice versa. To foreground the colonial condition of class relations in the Americas, I will use Peter Worsley's term *sub-proletariat* to identify the class location of those within and across racial/colonial groups who experience persistent cycles of unemployment or underemployment, possess little to no wealth, and struggle to maintain access to basic needs such as housing and food. The sub-proletariat names a particular position of economic inequality among and between the colonized at the same time as recognizing the colonizers' negation of the colonized's humanity.[2] Furthermore, it encourages an alliance between the urbanized peasantry and colonial/racial subjects from a variety of situations.[3] It is important to emphasize that this is not necessarily a static category, as class locations can sometimes change, but rather it names a people struggling in the coloniality of capitalist relations that stratifies access to resources along race, gender, and dis/ability lines. This builds on the insights of Chandra Mohanty regarding questions of racialized and gendered power relations, where the tendency to see all women in the "Third World" as a homogenous victimized group erases the class, ethnic, and geographic differences that stratify them.[4] bell hooks and Angela Davis have also argued that class now divides black women in the United States in a way that it did not during the time of explicit segregation. Both call for closer attention to class analyses in the contemporary moment.[5] At the same time, the ways in which colonialism has institutionalized unique social, psychological, and economic relations throughout the world calls for foregrounding the colonial/racial axis that also structures divisions between the sub-proletariat. To name this dual axis of race and class I will use the term *the damnés*. Importantly, this term does not forget the ways in which racism exceeds normative explanations of class as Fanon has compellingly demonstrated nor the ways in which class stratifies colonial/racial subjects.

The people of the damnés, as articulated by Fanon, encompasses the colonized of the world where there is a clear divide between the colonizers and the colonized. Fanon sees the colonized of the world in a common struggle with Europe and white European settlers. Wynter maintains the same Manichean division in her work that Fanon asserted, but further elaborates key specifics. Wynter's *Man* (the Western bourgeois ethnoclass) and *Native* are the two broad correlations to Fanon's colonizer and colonized, but the Native category has an internal hierarchy. The category of the Native encompasses all colonized peoples but specifies that those racialized as black occupy the nadir rung within this group.[6] Wynter's theorization clarifies the relationship between colonized peoples writ large and black positionality, a point that is unclear in Fanon's writings. It points out the hierarchal relationship between indigeneity and blackness, making it conceptually attentive to both "indigenous" and "black" as social positions, in addition to opening up a space for speaking of the "mixed-race" Black, Indian, or *casta* hacienda peón experience. The category of the damnés that Wynter denotes speaks to the way in which colonialisms and chattel slavery mutually constructed each other and continue to structure contemporary socioeconomic and intersubjective relations.[7] The Native category as articulated by Wynter facilitates speaking of not only the triadic schema of North America, but also of South America, as well as shifting differences between Africa and the Americas.

Issues of class hold an important significance for Wynter even though it is not always fully explained, as the damnés caught in the prison-industrial complex and the welfare state of the First World are both "part of the ever-expanding global, transracial category of the homeless/the jobless, the semi-jobless, the criminalized drug-offending prison population."[8] It is in a neighborhood specifically created by the welfare state where the "kicked about welfare moms" reside—a public housing project—that is where this chapter works toward a phenomenology of the damnés.

ON CLASS AS AN EMBODIED CONSCIOUSNESS

One's existence as part of the damnés provides important insights on themes such as hunger and homelessness that also creates particular possibilities of embodied consciousness. It is important to emphasize that the *insights* gleaned from the existence of the damnés are possibilities, never givens. Therefore, a methodological treatment and a set of theoretical concepts are necessary to examine the lived experience so that insights can be elaborated into a course of action.

"How did boring, white-bread Scarberia become Scarlem—a mess of street gangs, fire bombings and stabbings?" laments a *Toronto Life* article.[9] Another article quotes a Scarborough social worker: There "is a phenomenon called 'multi-daddying.' Teen moms are actually having more than one baby with various fathers as a way of forming bonds with new men in their lives."[10] There is a distinctly racialized and sexualized pattern of describing deindustrialized Scarborough that repeats in an incessant loop: "a crime-ridden area of greater Toronto known as the 'gang-infested wild, wild east'"; promiscuous, threatening.[11] The authors' words fix me with their gaze. They are the details, anecdotes, and stories from which they wove me and in which I critically stand.[12]

There is significant research that demonstrates the clear existence of neighborhood identities that are at once economic, racialized, and gendered.[13] In phenomenological terms, the damnés' neighborhood is the physical background from which residents face the world as well an object of consciousness to which residents are oriented. If consciousness is always oriented toward something, and in this case it is oriented toward a collection of buildings socially constructed as a neighborhood, then it is situated. Situated consciousness is necessarily embodied, historical, cultural, and sensitive. The relationship between one's raced, gendered, and classed embodiment and the collection of buildings in which one lives has an inherently social character. A perception of the buildings and of the self is necessarily shaped by the social situation in which the person exists. As people reflect on the buildings from different places in the world they take different positions toward the buildings, and each person is in turn also positioned in the world.[14] These different positions toward the buildings come not only from individualist, disembodied reflections, but from reflections that are necessarily in a social and embodied situation. It is from this line of inquiry that makes it clearer what is involved in stating that the existence of the damnés creates particular insights regarding the world that can lead to action. Their relationship to the buildings and the world are specifically situated. Furthermore, theoretical tools are needed to facilitate the examination of those insights to ensure that the actions taken do not fall into bad faith.

> I thought I was being asked to construct a physiological self, to balance space and localize sensations, when all the time they were clamoring for more.
>
> —Frantz Fanon

> Spaces acquire the "skin" of the bodies that inhabit them. What is important to note here is that it is not just bodies that are orientated. Spaces also take shape by being orientated around some bodies, more than others.
>
> —Sara Ahmed

Poverty impacts the embodied experience of space. It is important to state this because most theories of embodiment have been very good about explaining gender, race, and sex as embodied phenomenon, but class remains under-examined.[15] As philosopher Christine Overall has noted, "general references to class [in women's studies literature] are curiously empty of the experiential core that animates discussions of gender and race, 'and class' becomes the tail end of a litany that includes all the usual dimensions of oppression and marginalization, yet the inclusion of class remains theoretical."[16] In this account there is a form of economic relations, namely chronic unemployment, or precarious employment, that is operating. An elaboration of an example of how employment is experienced in a public housing community is elaborated below.

The inclusion of class as only a vague reference, but not an embodied experience is arguably one of the legacies of Frantz Fanon's book, *Black Skin, White Masks*. His thesis that antiblack racism exceeds the logic of class divisions has widely influenced the direction of theories of racial embodiment. However, Fanon would not say that capitalist relations are irrelevant, rather that they take different forms and require "stretching" Marx's theory of class in the colonial/racial context.[17] Specifically, Fanon understood "class differences" between the colonized as "the antagonism which exists between the native who is excluded from the advantages of colonialism and his counterpart who manages to turn colonial exploitation to his account."[18] Those who have difficulty turning colonialism to their benefit are, for example, the damnés with children escaping abusive relationships, the youth coming from those relationships, those with disabilities, felony records, or who are terminally ill, and seniors. Despite Fanon's legacy regarding discussions of race and class, the analysis he details in *Black Skin, White Masks* provides theoretical tools for elaborating the insights of the damnés (including on racialized and gendered class) into a plan of action.

For example, in a key section in *Being and Time*, Martin Heidegger discusses spatiality in such a way that Frantz Fanon can be read as taking particular issue. In short, there is a problem in the colonized world with the de-severance of Dasein that does not allow the colonial/racial subject to orient their Being-in-the-World with the "essential directionality of *Dasein*."[19] While Heidegger identifies the "bodily nature" as having a problematic of its own, he does not see it as necessary to elaborate this in his exposition of the relationship between Being-in-the-World and *Dasein*.[20] It is here that Fanon sees the crux of the colonial condition: the person of color has trouble elaborating his bodily schema. The expected dialectic between the body and the world is mediated with misanthropic effect by the "historical-racial schema" that actually attacks the "bodily nature" of the colonized (a nature that Heidegger takes for granted) and instead demands that the colonized/racialized body live in triplicate: being-in-itself/being-for-itself, being-for-others, and what can perhaps be referred to as being-for-the-vanished-other.[21] The vanished-other is evasive, hostile, transparent and absent.[22] When the colonial/racial body seeks to extend themselves in the spaces in which they inhabit through their critical thought and evaluations, their aesthetics, and nonnuclear family formations, they are instead confronted with stereotypes, hostility, and a repudiation of their intersubjectivity. This is not an absolute or totalizing social death as the antidialectics of space is describing the relationship between the colonized and the colonizer, between the damnés and Man. In contrast, social relations that entail reciprocal recognition can and do occur between and among the damnés.

ON SITUATED OPPOSITIONAL CONSCIOUSNESS

Situated oppositional consciousness, a form of consciousness organized in opposition to the dominant order by the colonized, can emerge from experiencing the world as part of the damnés. The experience of having one's humanity constantly questioned or outright negated can allow one to see the coloniality of the semiotic structure that one inhabits. Chela Sandoval calls this form of consciousness that necessarily involves an implicit affirmation of one's humanity and the rejection of dehumanization as the *methodology of the oppressed*. The methodology of the oppressed is the "field of force" that is "comprised of techniques for moving energy . . . both 'inner' or psychic technologies, and 'outer' technologies of social praxis."[23] The methodology of the oppressed is a form of embodied, self-reflective, actional, consciousness that is at once physiological, intellectual, psychological, spiritual, and social. What interests me here is examining what is involved in the existential enactment of oppositional consciousness.

Earlier, Chela Sandoval argues that what is needed to transform the individual's "field of force" into collective resistance is to successfully counter the colonization of meaning by ideology. The first step is to view one's experiences as a series of signs that can be read. Coming to see one's life as a web of symbols and meanings involves suspending the presumed knowledge one has of the world. For example, we can look at the category of "woman." On the one hand "woman" can be understood to be a part of nature's or God's division of the sexes. On the other hand, we can come to see "woman" as a category that requires the cognitive act of interpretation and that it is imbued with particular meanings. Sandoval's second step is to read the eidetic or cultural production as historical, the product of human agency, and imbued with power relations.[24] Sandoval refers to this step as deconstruction and Latina phenomenologist Jacqueline Martinez refers to it as critical judgment.

Martinez argues that critical judgment is necessary for "throwing off the inter-subjective pressures that would have persons of color believing the lie of their inferiority." Identifying colonial relations, slavery, and imperialism as structuring our current situations is from where critical judgment springs.[25] However, the inherent features of this identification process has not yet been fully detailed, the specifics of which reveal important insights for effecting social change.

It is in and through the process of coming to view one's world as a series of signs that can be read in addition to exercising critical judgment that Sandoval gives the special term "differential movement."[26] It involves being open to new possibilities, to approaching the world with a sense of wonder. This flexibility of consciousness holds a special importance in Sandoval's philosophy. She is clearly concerned with manifestations of rigidity in social movements, where individuals and/or organizations exhibit an unwillingness to see the world through the eyes of an other. Differential movement "is that which joins together the possible with what is"; the impetus for creating a new world.[27] Our facticity, the "what is" of our existences, is made up of the givens in our lives; our history, the languages we speak, the economic positions we hold, the race and gender we are identified as, even the choices we have made, and importantly *will* make. As beings with consciousness, we can "transcend" what is, go beyond our facticity. It is through our capacity as conscious beings that we can join what is with what is possible and avoid living in bad faith.

SPONTANEITY AS A FORM OF OPPOSITIONAL CONSCIOUSNESS

The remainder of this chapter is written in vignettes. Each vignette is a hermeneutic of a lived experience that, upon reflection, makes an important contribution toward a nascent sociogenic (the development of a person as a result of social factors) critical consciousness. A phenomenology of critical consciousness cannot be linear, nor comprehensive, but rather it is a methodology to illuminate embodied consciousness as it confronts decisions to make a choice and take an action.

The vignettes I offer here detail four distinct eidetic memories in a mode of self-reflection and critical judgment. The first is an encounter with a welfare worker in the effort to gain access to resources through social services. The second vignette is from the vantage point of living in public housing, detailing the embodied consciousness of class, gender, and race. From there I offer two more vignettes: one that seeks food through actions that are dominantly interpreted as petty crime, and the second that seeks food through a state-funded free lunch program.

ENCOUNTER WITH A WELFARE WORKER

> . . . because radical histories of working people are so invested in a materialist, workplace-centered understanding of class, it leaves very little space 'to discuss the development of class consciousness (as opposed to its expression) . . . '
>
> —Robin Kelley

This vignette examines the development of a racialized and gendered class consciousness. The scenario: she is an eleven-year-old child with the job of translating for her mother who is single with two children, in a telephone meeting with a welfare worker. She has learned that English is the language of power in this context, as not only are there no translation services available to facilitate these unscheduled efforts to access desperately needed resources, but she has witnessed how the tone and attitude chills when social service workers hear the heavy accent of someone struggling to speak English. The child has assessed that speaking grammatically correct in the local English dialect can make a world of difference between getting what one needs and being sent out empty-handed. The welfare worker speaks with a tone laced with suspicion, asking questions that make it clear they are going to assume you are a thief and a liar until you prove yourself otherwise. In these interactions the child sees themselves through the eyes of the government representative: dishonest, deficient, criminal, inferior. Shame mixed with indignance and anger fills the child for she knows her and her family's humanity and sees their hard work, determined efforts, and (as it turns out, misplaced) faith in the system. She is fully aware that there is a deeply unequal relation of power between her family and the welfare worker and has learned at an early age Fanon's insight: "To speak means to . . . grasp the morphology of this or that language, but it means above all to assume a culture, to support the weight of civilization."[28] The child makes an effort to not only learn the English language, but to wield it as a weapon. Her vocabulary will be infinite and her pronunciation immaculate; she will choose to use words that are esoteric and serrated. If the child can force the agent into a corner to either approve her request or be forced to admit he does not understand her vocabulary she will consider it a victory: Family 1, Welfare Worker 0.

These encounters between state agents or the managerial class and the members of the sub-proletariat profoundly shape their consciousness as they move through the world defined by an acute awareness of the sharp division of resources and justice. If the sub-proletariat in such a situation chooses to respond with defiant indignance, there emerges a form of consciousness that I will call "spontaneous oppositional consciousness" or "spontaneity."[29] This spontaneous form of oppositional consciousness is an organic radical response to sharp social divisions and an intuitive rejection of one's dehumanization. It asserts, sometimes forcefully, the humanity of the damnés. Fanon briefly discussed the oppositional consciousness of the damnés in *The Wretched of the Earth*, but I would argue that his description collapses what I am discerning here with another form of oppositional consciousness, what Chela Sandoval has termed "democratics." Fanon's description of the damnés' consciousness in the second chapter is not only what I have described as spontaneity, but it is also already oriented toward a collective effort beyond parrying with state workers and the managerial class on an individual level. In other words, there is a "we, the damnés" already collectively confronting their subjugation in what Fanon is describing.[30] It is a form of consciousness that Fanon ascribed the possibility of reactionary politics, but also the potential to be a radically revolutionary force.[31] In Sandoval's terms, what Fanon describes is a "field of force" oriented toward democratics. Spontaneous oppositional consciousness, on the other hand, is implicit to Fanon's theory; but is not identified in its specificity. It is a crucial aspect of an oppositional consciousness that is central to spontaneous street rebellions that rise like a fire in response to an injustice.

From where does spontaneous oppositional consciousness well? Fanon speaks of the need for liberation among the damnés as biological.[32] Sylvia Wynter expands on this notion and states that the conception of the human we are now living by is a *biodicy*.[33] What they are arguing is that the redefinition of the human in racial terms, with only Man as its full beneficiary, is fundamentally about who gets to live and who prematurely dies; who is perceived as invaluable and who is cut off from the communion of Man. What I am emphasizing here is that the struggle over basic needs in the encounter with a welfare worker is a struggle over life and death. The spontaneous form of oppositional consciousness that emerges from this struggle is fundamentally about survival, it does not emerge from an elaborated political program. Rather, the spontaneous form of oppositional consciousness must be connected with a methodological treatment to elaborate insights into a course of action. It is from subjecting spontaneity to a methodological treatment that the possibility of other forms of oppositional consciousness will emerge. What is key to understand here is that the embodied experience of moving through the social order will shape and inform the conclusions drawn from an engagement with a methodological analysis. The conclusions drawn will shape and inform the course of action that one takes. Political tendencies do not emerge from a disembodied intellectualism, but rather are possibilities based on insights gleaned from the lived experience examined under a methodological treatment.

As the reader can see, spontaneous oppositional consciousness is not a predetermined political program nor an organized social movement, for the rebellions that emerge from this form of consciousness need to be oriented in another direction. It is at this point that many forms of consciousness can emerge. "Equal rights," "revolutionary," "supremacist," "separatist," and "differential," are five that Sandoval has identified, for which I am differentiating a precondition: "spontaneity." I detail this form of consciousness to challenge the dismissal of spontaneous rebellions as necessarily counterproductive and the relegation of the sub-proletariat to an easily co-opted reactionary social class. I also detail it to make clear that the insurgent affirmation of one's humanity can be further oriented toward a reactionary politics, but there is no type of human being who is intrinsically "socially conservative," "reformist," and so forth. Rather, the revolutionary effort needs to be toward connecting spontaneous oppositional consciousness to a methodological analysis that will evade bad faith and shape the road to action.

THE NEIGHBORHOOD OF THE DAMNÉS

"I don't think it's really a color issue, I think it's more of a bias issue. . . . It [skin color] doesn't affect me when I'm looking for a job at all because I just use a different address. That's what really deters you from getting a job." I was struck by these sentences when I read them in an online newspaper. I had grown accustomed to reading news articles and academic studies that failed to capture the contradictions of public housing residents (we are either heroes or villains, rarely contradictory, desiring actors), but here was a statement in a news media forum that caught me by surprise. The statement sharpened a memory of my own about living in public housing: being from certain neighborhoods in Scarborough was a fact to be hidden from potential employers. On reflection, it can be said that living in public housing can overdetermine one's perception of the world.

Before overwhelming the above quote with a critique that immediately asserts the primacy of race or affirms the correctness of the class-first position for understanding socioeconomic situations, I want to pause at the apprehension of pathways of possibility, as well as obstacles, being implicitly described. I want to take it as an opportunity to demonstrate that the decolonial methodology can be helpful and necessary for elaborating the insights from the lived experience of the damnés into actions that are not prey to bad faith.

The statement above was made by Melody McClymont, a resident of the Kingston-Galloway housing projects in Scarborough, in response to the question, "Where do you hope to be in 5 years?" The 2013 interview was part of a news piece on the persistence of poverty in Scarborough and contains a full video recording of the exchange.[34] It is interesting that a residential address is foregrounded in perceptions of possible and impossible futures. McClymont talks at length about how her home address in Kingston-Galloway is the major obstacle to her employment opportunities and future goals. As a young black woman and single mother, her statement highlights something underexamined but crucial about the experience of living in public housing: living in a housing project structures the relationship between the self and the world in a crucial way that delineates one's encounters with others. "The projects" come to be identified as a locus of the experience of being denied one's humanity. Stereotypes obstruct residents from establishing relationships with potential employers, the very relationship that would supposedly deliver them from their circumstances. As I looked deeper into this insight, I found research on residents of the *banlieus* in France and the ghettos of Chicago that state "discrimination based on one's address hampers the job search and contributes to entrenching local unemployment as residents . . . encounter additional distrust and reticence among employers as soon as they mention where they live."[35] This phenomenon was termed "territorial stigmatization" and its effects are not relegated only to interactions with employers, but also "with the police, the courts and street-level bureaucracies such as the state unemployment and welfare offices, all of which are especially prompt to modify their conduct and procedures based on residence. . . . All youths recount the change of attitude of policemen when they notice their address during identity checks."[36] A resident may be a colonial/racial subject that has been racially profiled, but is now *one of those kinds* of colonial/racial subjects. There are material and subjective differences within the spatiality of the damnés and to not make those differences a systematic component of a critical analyses only raises the suspicion of those who are "territorially stigmatized."[37]

An examination of the experience of racialized and gendered class in public housing as a *situation* reveals an important aspect of being of the sub-proletariat: one's neighborhood is experienced as an extension of the historical-racial schema that lies "beneath the body schema."[38] The resident's sense of self and the physical buildings in which they live are mutually constituting. McClymont's statement reveals a crucial point about the phenomenal body in the colonial/racial context: each object that makes up a cultural world is imbued with the logic of colonial relations, from the imagination and careful measurements of those who designed the buildings, to the touch of the hands of the people who arranged the furniture inside the apartments. Those whose behavior patterns settle into what is taken as the nature of the buildings forms the cultural world through which the residents move.

In the presence of another person, ideally the other is aware of them as a conscious being that is looking back at them and recognizes that there is a world that the other sees from their unique vantage point. The same is reciprocated when the other person returns their look. This recognition of the other is our insertion into the world as an individual and reveals that spatiality is fundamentally social. In a colonial context, however, the social is stratified and antiblack.

The behavior patterns of the people in a colonial world structure the physical world, imbuing objects with a particular semiotic code. Objects, such as the buildings that make up a public housing complex, are molded to serve Man's image of the world, and thus the residents are entering the buildings within an established code of social relations. "The housing projects" are already within a system of racialized, gendered, and classed signs that ascribe a particular meaning to the place, which in this case is stigmatized. The socially sedimented codes of race, gender, class, and ability are already present at the residents' arrival to the buildings.

As for the residents' explicit consciousness of visible race, gender, class, and disability as structure—the preconditions that make being assigned public housing possible—can be in the background as vague or unclear stimuli under the everyday conditions of seeking to improve one's access to resources. This may account for the secondary role of race and the unmentioned role of gender that McClymont ascribes to her economic struggles. What is a clear and distinct stimulus in the accounts of the residents of a stigmatized neighborhood is the noted difference in attitude that resident's experience in their encounters with employers, police officers, and other state officials. The encounter with this difference in attitude is the situation that transforms the pre-conscious relationships with race, gender, class, and ability, into a definite reckoning with one's facticity. This way in which the reckoning manifests as an explicitly hood-oriented consciousness is perhaps not ideal to the social scientist, but it is nevertheless a reality. It is in and through being confronted with territorial stigma that can be an important part of the focus of residents' consciousness regarding unequal power relations and dehumanization. This is an important insight as it should influence organizing efforts to connect the particularities of racialized and gendered class consciousness to an analysis of social structures and a praxis of social change.

In a colonial/racial context, the complex of buildings in which the damnés live has not receded into a background that must be compelled to consciousness from a pre-conscious background as is the case for the middle classes. Rather, the signs that specify the location of one's home, such as an address, is foregrounded in encounters with other people, to the point that it overdetermines the sense of possibilities for residents. What accounts for the territorial stigma that enlivens the orientation of the residents' consciousness? Racism, capitalism, and the colonial gender system. How, then, does a cluster of buildings, the sidewalks, and the streets themselves, become imbued with negative stereotypes?

It has been said that the objects in the physical world spread round each of them an atmosphere of humanity which may be determinant in a high or low degree.[39] The meaning of this can be understood in an examination of the personality ascribed to the dwellings of the damnés. Think for a moment of the emotional reactions toward spaces designated as "the projects." The empty sidewalks, the still windows, and the facades of brown or red brick are imbued with a particular personality. They are, even when empty with no signs of movement, often perceived as threatening, aggressive, and dangerous. The physical world where the damnés dwell, the objects around them—stairwells, elevators, hallways—are patterned into the social schema exactly as the residents have been. The buildings themselves are not anonymous things out there separate from residents and onlookers but are imbued with the same dehumanized qualities as the residents. This not only introduces a negation of recognition between the damnés and the colonizer but introduces a new kind of relationship between the damnés and the physical world. The damnés correctly perceive that they are cast as racialized objects among racialized objects. Thus, the identification between the residents and the buildings shape their situation, and there is a recognition that the "civilization in which I play my part exists for me in a self-evident way in the implements with which it provides itself."[40] In a colonial/racial context, these objects are not only rendered as an extension of the damné's body but are animated as racialized objects just as they are. Quiet sidewalks, empty elevators, and lonely stairwells come alive with the stereotypes of the people who inhabit them: menacing, aggressive, hypersexual, and threatening.

The beneficiaries of colonialism, including the colonized who have managed to turn the colonial project to their benefit, do not want to face the sub-proletariat nor the places in which they dwell to confront the terror of what has been created and continues to be replicated. The implications of this are not only for the relationship between the colonized and the colonizers, but also between the damnés. Housing project residents that do not recognize that the negation of their own humanity, as well as that of their physical and cultural world, are the creation of the social world that they have inherited are likely to have one of two responses: either seek to flee the stigmatized territory and seek acceptance in the white world (sadistic bad faith), or come to identify uncritically with the stigmatized territory (masochistic bad faith). Both responses are definitively in bad faith, so what is to be done?

Rather than assume that residents can only choose one or the other form of bad faith, residents can affirm the awareness of not being identical to the objects upon which we reflect. Affirming one's humanity becomes critical here. What does it mean to be human? To be human is not to be a particular kind of species, but rather to be a relationship. To be a relationship that is responsive and responsible for the well-being of all people, particularly those experiencing even further subjugation than ourselves. The key is not to become one with what the nonresident sees.[41] It is in the effort to take responsibility for the well-being of all, particularly those most subjugated, that joining others in a collective becomes important. The collective can both elaborate a plan of action as well as reaffirm being human in relation, rather than simply an object among objects that endlessly seeks money in a meaningless existence.

Rather than push or pull on the primacy of class or race in response to Melody McClymont's statement or my own memories of identification, I pursued an analysis that sought to understand what it is about living in a housing project that strongly defines the lived experience of those who live in them. It is an aspect of the consciousness of the damnés that is clearly expressed and well represented in neighborhood-based identities and in popular media, from spray painted wall tags to radio host shout outs but is underexamined as an orientation in scholarship on working-class consciousness. There is a curious phenomenon of having a strong sense of neighborhood pride among those who grow up in "the projects" all the while knowing that residing in particular neighborhoods is not only representative of one's economic subjugation, but actually presents definitive obstacles to one's future economic and social possibilities. Rather than critique the perspective that territorial stigma is an issue separate from or above race, or assert a class-first analysis, I took "hood consciousness" as speaking to a perspective that reveals an important insight. Once examined through a decolonial methodology it was revealed that the damnés identify with the territorially stigmatized neighborhoods in which we dwell precisely because of the negation of the self/other relationship in the colonial/racial context and the irreducible relationship between physical objects, the social/cultural world, and the orientation of consciousness. Pushing the insights of the damnés in and through contradictions can lead to an analysis that will resonate more strongly with the experiences of the damnés and facilitate connecting spontaneity with other forms of oppositional consciousness toward action that do not fall into bad faith.

In the next two sections I examine two instances of what Sandoval describes as "leading a consuming consciousness away from the sense of meaning-as-nature" toward the possibilities of effecting change.[42]

CRIMINALITY, SPONTANEITY, AND POLITICAL CONSCIOUSNESS IN A LIFE OF THE *DAMNÉS*

They were a ragamuffin group of youth, tough and wise beyond their years, yet naïve with the illusion of an impossible immortality. One was fourteen and the others were a few years older. As a crew of young women strolling in a downtown Toronto neighborhood with no money, but plenty of mischief, they showed a brash bravery that was out of place in a world that bullied them with sexual and gendered violence. They noticed the open basement window to the kitchen of a community center and decided to jump in and look for some food to eat. They searched all the cupboards and fridge but found only empty shelves. There was an object out of place in the orange laminate kitchen: a cardboard box full of books. They were not happy about leaving empty-handed, so they shoved a copy of the book in their jackets before climbing back out onto the street. Bored and hungry they planted themselves on a building stoop and looked at the book they found. It was called *The Creation of World Poverty* by Teresa Hayter. Flipping through the pages, one of the young women of color could feel her consciousness open to the world she faced. She could not understand all the words and did not know all the references being made, but that did not bar her from gaining a new perspective. She suddenly learned that poverty was not because of bad luck or being cursed, as she had thought her family was, but was systemic and maintained by particular institutions operating on a global level. It was equally amazing to her that someone had been able to pierce through the fog of self-effacement that poverty tends to induce and reveal a crack in the system: that it was man-made and changeable. That night, she learned for the first time about the concept of structure and had her first sense of the libratory potential of scholarship.

The life-world she inhabited prior to opening the pages of that book and after, changed enormously.[43] Prior to that experience, poverty and various forms of subjugation were a part of her world as existence-as-nature. The indignation she felt against her dehumanization, the spontaneous consciousness I described above, did not provide an explicit accounting of the world that would denaturalize poverty or racialized/gendered subjugation in her reflections on the world. She was unable to engage in a revolution, but upon reading the words describing the capitalist system that explicitly discussed colonialism and underdevelopment, her worldview was unsettled. It is not the only way that denaturalization could have happened, but it is important to trace how class consciousness finds new orientations among the *damnés* in First World contexts. She could not have known that breaking into a building would change her reflective world. It is also in this banal sense that Jean Paul-Sartre means "we are our actions." She cannot predict her future based exclusively on her past because previously unknown dimensions of the world are revealed to her through her actions. We cannot know a priori what a "decolonized" world will look like because our actions and those of others create the possibilities for what the world will be. The effort to feed herself, despite not having any money or anything to barter or trade, resulted with renewing "the symbols, the myths, the beliefs, the emotional responsiveness" toward poverty.[44] There is no way she could have anticipated that.

This account of a first exposure to a systematic description and critique of capitalism reveals the inherent struggle for the *damnés*. She was able to connect her personal experience to a structural analysis and thus shift her individual consciousness by engaging in a "criminal" act. Stealing to feed herself could have ended with her arrest and a sentence to juvenile detention. This experience foregrounds the conflict and definitive struggle between those who own private property, the state, and poor women of color as they become actional. The point here is that as human beings we are always in a process of becoming, and the world that the damnés face turns all agency to address their social conditions into a crime. This realization points to the need for structural change.

ENCOUNTER WITH FREE LUNCH PROGRAM PROVIDERS

> [P]oetry reaches back through the levels of meaning production to try to lead consciousness out of its disciplinization and inscription in culture to a potential utopia.
>
> —Chela Sandoval

> The [free breakfast for schoolchildren] program will raise consciousness in the form of people participating in a program that they put together themselves to serve themselves and their children. . . . The consciousness of the children will be raised in that they will see someone outside the structure of their own family working in their interest and motivated by love and concern.
>
> —Black Panther Party

> Direct support is premised on the notion that supporting people in fighting for their most basic needs, especially to live in safety, is necessary in advancing the struggle.
>
> —Harsha Walia

At the busy intersection of Markham and Ellesmere there were bus stops on every corner. Scarborough is in the northeast corner of Toronto, so most people at the time headed south or west. To get to school, work, or go see the *Rocky Horror Picture Show*, she had to get on the Markham Road 102 bus. The bus route was about thirty-five minutes to the subway, so her routine was to read a book there and back, and her lunch or dinner was often a spicy Jamaican patty at the bakery in Warden Station. They were warm on a winter day and only cost something like a dollar (they're $1.25 now). It was on this and other buses that she read books like Malcolm X's *Autobiography*, George Orwell's *Animal Farm*, and Margaret Atwood's *A Handmaid's Tale*. The practice of reading for a minimum of an hour and a half a day from the age of fourteen on would pay off later when she stumbled into college as a "nontraditional" student. She never finished high school, but she was well-read and a disciplined reader as a result of this routine.

"These people don't need poetry, they need food," Milton Acorn, a well-known Communist poet, declared at the end of a poetry class at Contact Alternative High School. It was the early 1980s in the heart of Regent Park, a downtown housing project racialized as Indian (of the Americas), now referred to as "Neighbourhood Improvement Area #72," and the distracted students couldn't focus on his abstractions over the rumble of their stomachs. The average age of the students at Contact was nineteen and many were returning to get their high school diploma after experiencing an unforgiving job market amid neoliberal reforms.[45] It was upon Acorn's observation that a self-identifying Communist, proposed a free breakfast and lunch program for students. With full support from the Contact staff, funds were successfully secured from the Toronto District School Board and free breakfasts and lunches were provided from then on. There was no other program like it in the city. In a context of immense hostility and suspicion directed toward the poor and the tendency to erase the experience of poverty in the First World, to have the workers of a particular organization acknowledge that there were hungry people in the midst of so much settler colonial wealth produced an experience similar to that of being recognized by a stranger. Given that subjectivity is constituted by interhuman contact, if negation and erasure is the normative experience, to have the experience of being seen also illuminates a path to action. The shame that usually accompanied discussions of her family's material conditions was curiously absent in this encounter. Being seen, one returns the look and a new sense of the self as a socially connected being flashes.

The program to address hunger was integrated into the curriculum so instead of discussing a newspaper article or poem, the English class provided the space to organize and talk about the food program's logistics and politics: What would the menu for the week be? Were the meals nutritious and affordable? What groceries needed to be purchased? Were the meals easy to cook and serve for close to two hundred students? Menus that would appeal to a wide variety of palates had to be created, grocery shopping trips organized, cooking and cleaning tasks agreed to, and all tasks needed to be successfully executed. Consensuses needed to be reached, roles and responsibilities needed to be delegated, accepted, and carried out. And we needed to return each day, face-to-face, resolve conflicts, and do our part to keep feeding everyone. Although the funds for the program were from the settler state, the program still managed to initiate a culture of politics through the way the program was implemented. A relationship of responsiveness and responsibility was created by the teachers, student services staff, and students in a context otherwise void of the ethical treatment of the damnés.

To address an issue that undercuts and circumvents your well-being through a collective effort is a revolutionary experience. The dialectical relationship between efforts to change your world and changing yourself cannot be emphasized enough. The experience not only changes the consciousness of self among those involved with directly taking action to address their poverty, but it changes the consciousness of the issues themselves. The victory was tangible in this effort: to ease the immediate hunger of the students and to know that future meals were certain and reliable. Now, instead of wondering if subjugation and hunger were a part of the natural order, she as a young organizer came to understand that resources had been deliberately denied. A tangible connection between what *The Creation of World Poverty* stated regarding the underdevelopment thesis and the politics of the free breakfast/lunch program made a concrete connection in her thinking.

The staff at contact were explicitly and unapologetically political. Self-identified anarchists, Communists, Irish revolutionaries, and queer feminists were the norm. The school curriculum fleshed out the politics of the lunch program and was unlike any other in Toronto: black studies, Native (indigenous) studies, LGBT literature, and world religions, were a few of the options students had. A significant aspect of the school was the way students were integrated into the decision making and curriculum-building for the school. The entire school of two hundred students would get together periodically to discuss and vote on course offerings. They were exposed to many books at this time that would shape her political awareness, but the book that set her on a different trajectory was *Malcolm X's Autobiography*. His cutting insights on colorism, the symbiosis between patriarchal violence, domestic abuse, and white supremacy, the enormous challenges his mother faced, intraracial class divisions, and antiblack racism spurred a critical synthesis of her own world. There were and are enormous differences between Trinidad, Mexico City, Toronto, and the state of Georgia, but there are also structural connections. A demystification process began, and she understood that suffering was no longer something to react to but to act on. Malcolm X taught her that the lived experience of the *damnés* was an accounting of Western civilization that had been deliberately written out of the record.

She became more politically conscious, that is to say, oriented toward deciphering individual struggles in terms of structural conditions and constraints. To this end, part of the process is coming to understand where one stands not only in relation to whiteness, but in relation to other colonial/racial subjects. "What are you?" was a question that dogged her. In a context where one is expected to be able to identify as one category, (white, black, First Nation, Arab, or Asian) saying she was half Trinidadian and half Mexican never seemed to really answer the question. When she told a teacher at Contact she wanted to learn more about her Mexican history, he suggested going to the Toronto Indian Friendship Center so that she could hopefully access a decolonial history. Despite what she learned there, the nagging need to be able to answer the identity question in normative terms continued to nag her. The inability to choose one and only one identity as it seemed most everyone was able to claim felt to her like a deficiency, like she needed to be able to answer the question with one word. She turned to mixed race literature and found many of the themes addressed there. She read extensively on miscegenation and the consistent themes of blues and tragedy. She read how racial identity could itself be a form of bad faith.[46] She also read its converse, how not identifying as black and/or indigenous was colonial and antiblack.[47] The demands for a normative either/or identity that correlated with visible race in political organizing and the ways in which her lived experience refused to cooperate with those demands remained to be adequately addressed.

The examination of the existential enactment of oppositional consciousness in a public housing complex in a colonial context raises the question of the relationship between race and class. In a normative understanding of race, there is the presence or absence of particular biological facts: skin color, hair texture, toe shape, a birthmark, and so forth. In this logic, the absence or presence of certain markers is evidence of a race.[48] Identity is expected to correlate with the bodily markers. However, as I have written elsewhere, alleles can be patterned differently and unpredictably across siblings, even twins, revealing that there are no definitive sets of properties.[49] Poet and playwright Langston Hughes based his 1925 play, *Mulatto*, on this very theme. The assumption that what is real functions as a mind independent set of properties that apply to all members of a racial group cannot account for the siblings that appear visibly different from each other. Furthermore, one would assume that the long history of mixed race people would complicate the notion that people can be of one and only one racial group at a time, over the course of their lifetime. However, in practice, even when the children are given a different racial category that is supposed to account for their being mixed, such as mulata or mestiza, they, too, function as categories that presume a set of mind independent properties that are evidence of that particular race. How did we get to this place in our assumptions about being in the world? We turn to that question now.

NOTES

1. Jean Paul Sartre, *Critique of Dialectical Reason, Volume One* (New York: Verso, 1960); Simon J. Charlesworth, *A Phenomenology of Working-Class Experience* (Cambridge: Cambridge University Press, 2000).

2. Peter Worsley, "Frantz Fanon and the 'Lumpenproletariat,'" *The Socialist Register* 9 (1972): 208.

3. Worsley, 211.

4. Chandra Talpade Mohanty, "Under Western Eyes: Feminist Scholarship and Colonial Discourses," *boundary* 2, Vol. 12, no. 3, On Humanism and the University I: The Discourse of Humanism (Spring–Autumn 1984): 55.

5. bell hooks, *Where We Stand: Class Matters*; Angela Davis, *Blues Legacies and Black Feminism* (New York: Vintage Books, 1998).

6. Wynter, "Unsettling the Coloniality of Being/Power/Truth/Freedom: Towards the Human, After Man, Its Overrepresentation—An Argument," *CR: The New Centennial Review* 3, no. 3 (2003): 257–337.

7. Wynter builds on Anibal Quijano's concept of coloniality. See Aníbal Quijano, "Coloniality and Modernity/Rationality," *Cultural Studies* 21, no. 2–3 (2007): 168–78.

8. Ibid., 261.

9. Don Gillmor, "The Scarborough Curse." *Toronto Life*, December 1, 2007. Accessed July 28, 2016. http://torontolife.com/city/the-scarborough-curse/. See also, News Staff, "Scarborough Tries to Clear Its 'Crime' Rep," *CityNews*, January 10, 2007. Accessed July 28, 2016. http://www.citynews.ca/2007/01/10/scarborough-tries-to-clear-its-crime-rep/.

10. Cathy Gulli, "Suddenly Teen Pregnancy Is Cool?" *Macleans.ca*, January 17, 2008. Accessed July 28, 2016. https://www.ywcatoronto.org/upload/media-2008 Suddenly teen pregnancy cool.pdf.

11. "Dwayne's World." *Dwayne's World*, 2010. Accessed July 28, 2016. http://www.thescottishsun.co.uk/scotsol/homepage/sport/spl/3321720/Dwaynes-world.html.

12. Frantz Fanon, *Black Skin, White Masks* (New York: Grove Press, 2008).

13. Tricia Rose, *Black Noise: Rap Music and Black Culture in Contemporary America* (Hanover, NH: University Press of New England, 1994); Murray Forman, *The 'Hood Comes First: Race, Space, and Place in Rap and Hip-Hop* (Middletown, CT: Wesleyan University Press, 2002); Benjamin Looker, *A Nation of Neighborhoods: Imagining Cities, Communities, and Democracy in Postwar America* (Chicago: The University of Chicago Press, 2015).

14. Sara Ahmed, *Queer Phenomenology: Orientations, Objects, Others* (Durham, NC: Duke University Press, 2006), 28.

15. Simon J. Charlesworth, *A Phenomenology of Working-Class Experience* (Cambridge: Cambridge University Press, 2000).

16. Christine Overall, "Nowhere at Home: Toward a Phenomenology of Class Consciousness," in *This Fine Place So Far from Home: Voices of Academics from the Working Class*, ed. Carlos L. Dews, 209–20 (Philadelphia: Temple University Press, 1995, 212).

17. See his critique of the Marxist definition of the lumpenproletariat and the role of the working class in Frantz Fanon, *The Wretched of the Earth* (New York: Grove/Atlantic, Inc., 2007). Also, see comment in Frantz Fanon, *Black Skin, White Masks* (New York: Grove Press, 2008), 89, 193, 205.

18. Frantz Fanon, *The Wretched of the Earth* (New York: Grove/Atlantic, Inc., 2007), 112.
19. Martin Heidegger, *Being and Time* (New York: Harper, 1962), 144.
20. Ibid., 143.
21. Fanon, *Black Skin, White Masks*, 91–92.
22. Ibid., 92.
23. Chela Sandoval, *Methodology of the Oppressed* (Minneapolis: University of Minnesota Press, 2000), 82.
24. Sandoval, *Methodology*, 101–02.
25. Jacqueline M. Martinez, *Phenomenology of Chicana Experience and Identity: Communication and Transformation in Praxis* (Lanham, MD: Rowman & Littlefield, 2000), 90.
26. Sandoval, *Methodology*, 104.
27. Ibid., 180.
28. Frantz Fanon, *Black Skin, White Masks* (New York: Grove Press, 2008), 1–2.
29. Sandoval, *Methodology of the Oppressed*, 44.
30. Fanon, *Wretched*, 130. For example, he states, "These workless less-than-men are rehabilitated in their own eyes and in the eyes of history. The prostitutes too, and the maids who are paid two pounds a month, all the hopeless dregs of humanity, all who turn in circles between suicide and madness, will recover their balance, once more go forward, and march proudly in the great procession of the awakened nation."
31. Fanon, *Wretched*, 129.
32. Ibid., 130.
33. Sylvia Wynter, "On How We Mistook the Map for the Territory, and Reimprisoned Ourselves in Our Unbearable Wrongness of Being, of Desêtre: Black Studies Toward the Human Project," in *A Companion to African-American Studies*, ed. Lewis R. Gordon and Jane Anna Gordon (Malden, MA: Blackwell Publishing, 2006), 107–18.
34. James Armstrong and Patrick Cain, "Income Mapped: Long After 'Priority' Designation, Pockets of Poverty Persist in East Scarborough," *Global News*, July 3, 2013. Accessed July 28, 2016. http://globalnews.ca/news/690882/scarborough-income-map/.
35. Loïc J. D. Wacquant, *Urban Outcasts: A Comparative Sociology of Advanced Marginality* (Cambridge: Polity Press, 2008).
36. Ibid., 174.
37. I raise Wacquant's ethnography here not to shift to a sociological analysis nor to center the work of Bourdieu and Wacquant, but rather to center the interviews that were conducted with public housing residents to affirm the scope of the discussion here.
38. Fanon, *Black Skin, White Masks*, 91.
39. Maurice Merleau-Ponty, *Phenomenology of Perception* (New York: Routledge, 2004), 405.
40. Ibid.
41. Lewis Gordon, *Bad Faith and Antiblack Racism* (Amherst, NY: Humanity Press, 1995).

42. Sandoval, *Methodology*, 103.

43. "Life-world" refers to the naively experienced, immediately perceived reality of everyday life as grasped and understood by individuals in the midst of their ordinary activities. Maurice Natanson, *The Journeying Self: A Study in Philosophy and Social Role* (Boston: Addison-Wesley, 1970), 95.

44. Frantz Fanon, *A Dying Colonialism* (New York: Grove Press, 1967), 30.

45. Steve Moore, personal communication with author, August 6, 2015.

46. Naomi Zack, *Race and Mixed Race* (Philadelphia: Temple University Press, 1993).

47. Jared Sexton, *Amalgamation Schemes: Antiblackness and the Critique of Multiculturalism* (Minneapolis: University of Minnesota Press, 2008); Guillermo Bonfil Batalla, *Mexico Profundo: Reclaiming a Civilization* (Austin: The University of Texas Press, 1996).

48. Michael Monahan, *The Creolizing Subject* (New York: Fordham University Press, 2011), 108–109.

49. Daphne Taylor-García, "'Mixed' Existence: On Rachel Dolezal and Alleles," in *The Feminist Wire*, August 13, 2015.

Chapter 2

Visible Race and the Legacy of the *Sistema de Castas*

There is a mode of hailing people in Latinx and Latin American vernacular that instantly imbues the atmosphere with a particular way of classifying morphology. "*Güera*, que la vendemos, *güera*!" the vendors at Saturday's *mercado del Cerro del Judio* in Mexico City or *Tenochtitlan*, would call to me. Pausing at the various *puestos* to purchase fruit and vegetables, housewares or prepared foods I would be absorbed in assessing the ripeness of the *tunas*, how long the line was for the blue corn *huaraches*, or if there was anything I needed to take back with me to Canada or the United States. In those moments, my consciousness was fully oriented toward my actions and my body "followed" behind as if invisible. But the calls of "güera!" would snap my consciousness toward my self as an object in the other's eyes, and I would momentarily lose sight of the ears of corn or brown clay bowls and be focused on what my morphology appeared to those around me. It was sharply different than what I experienced in California. The encounters were not the equivalent of a "hey, you!" for they foregrounded my skin tone and gender as the mode of delineating me from the people around me that they did not refer to by the same name. And it wasn't the same as being a tourist because many of the people around me were my relatives; the neighborhood was home to at least four generations of my family. Implicitly and instantaneously, it was a mode of classifying me and those around me between light and dark.

I looked over my skin, my hair, my coloring, and discovered the *sistema de castas* and a history of lactification. The commonplace usage of words like *güera*, *morena*, *prieto* in Mexico underscored the normality of openly referring to people by their skin tone and gendered appearance that paralleled the West Indian norms of my father's maternal side of the family. Trinidad's black, brown, red, spanish, and so forth, was *negrita/o*, *prieta/o*, *morena/o*, *güera/o*, etc. in Mexico. This phenomenon in the Latin American context can be referred to as colorism. The specific names given to different colors differ from region to region, and sometimes different values are attributed to the same body in different places, but the *logic* for identifying others is the same: a hierarchal reading of morphology. What was this practice, why was it used, and where did it come from? We know from Foucault that the emerging sciences of the classical episteme in Europe understood knowledge primarily as a practice of ordering and classifying on the basis of essential differences.[1] The classification of humans as morphological types with distinct constitutions was one of the conclusions drawn and popularized by the likes of Carl Linnaeus. But how did the intellectual production of European scientists turn into everyday modes of relating to others in Spanish colonies?

The semiotic structures of the cultures we live in are not only intellectual constructs but social and economic ones that enable and constrain our very perceptions of other people as well as our own selves, and they constitute our modes of communication. For the most part, the lexicon with which we speak is rarely the object of analysis, but it is possible to shift our practice of speaking from operating in the natural attitude to an object of analysis. Suspending the words we use to refer to one another, examining their meanings, as well as the conditions in which they are used allows us to understand the unconscious relationships that are being forged by our words on a daily basis. It can help us better see and understand how colorism is practiced and maintained, and thus provide insights on how to make interventions.

This chapter focuses on the ontological assumptions implicit to the *sistema de castas* as a system of classification and social control that fused morphology into a hierarchal division of labor. An etiology of the *sistema de castas* can be illuminated through a reading of Plato's metaphysics. Reading colonial narratives through Plato provides important details about the lexicon used to classify "mixed peoples." Platonism is a key part of European Christianity's cultural and intellectual foundation, and the Spanish colonial project was the means of its development from a local history to a global design.[2] Several scholars have written about the ontology of black, red, yellow, and white racialization, but the specifics of the people who are deemed of "mixed" lineage has not been equally explained. The *sistema de castas* was developed over the course of the sixteenth through eighteenth centuries and officially ended in 1821, but the underlying logic continues to shape Latinx racial consciousness today. The effort here is "to make visible the practices of visibility itself, to outline the background from which our knowledge of others and of ourselves appears in relief," so that we may be able to alter the associated meanings ascribed to visible difference as well as the ontological assumptions that underlie those meanings.[3] Thus, the purpose of this project is not to sediment "castas" or "mixed race" as determinative categories, but rather to elucidate their construction and to then resituate the human.

THE "MIXING" OF BLACK, RED, AND WHITE

The negation of a full expression of being-for-others in a colonial world is what leads Fanon to identify a historical-racial-schema that operates "below the corporeal schema." It is a colonial schema that maintains antiblack racism and also encompasses the racialization of colonized people as not-black/not-white. Sylvia Wynter has elaborated this historical-racial-schema as the founding *triadic schema* between black, red, and white racial groups. The conclusions she draws regarding the values ascribed to each of the three categories rest on her reflections on sociological and humanities research on the existence of black and indigenous peoples over the past five hundred years, including the work of Anthony Pagden. Pagden delineated that the triadic schema as a hierarchy between natural slaves (black), nature's children (red), and fully human (white). His findings were based on excavating the deep influence that the writings of Aristotle had on Spanish colonists' theorization of the human in the colonial context. What has not been specifically addressed by Wynter nor Pagden was the fourth broad category that was produced under colonialism: *castas*. In this chapter I demonstrate that "mixed" people, including Afro-castas, were produced as distinct categories of people using the same Platonic rationale and thus not subsumable to red, white, or black in the Spanish colonial context as in the US context. Furthermore, reading the conditions in which the language of "being mixed" emerged through Plato and the Stoics and interpreted in the colonial context, I reveal the ontological assumptions that make being both/and of two or more racial categories a threat to Man (as that which is currently overrepresenting the human). Plato and the Stoics provided Spanish colonists with a template with which to elaborate the social location of *castas* in the triadic labor schema and to delineate a relationship between red, white, black, and variously "mixed" people. Knowing this important aspect of the Spanish colonial racial schema provides the damnés with one specific locus on how to alter the meanings ascribed to visible race.

The theoretical analysis for examining colorism and intersubjectivity that animates this chapter is from Frantz Fanon's *Black Skin, White Masks*. In the book, Fanon narrates a first-person encounter in Paris: "Dirty nigger!" or simply, "Look, a Negro!"[4] These encounters seal the black person in a state of objecthood and, Fanon observes, are constitutive of social relations in a colonized society. The seal is a negation of the form of consciousness that should ideally emerge in the presence of others: being-for-others. Being-for-others is an aspect of being in the world that can be identified when one looks at other conscious beings and they look back. Before reflecting on being looked at, one experiences a profound shift of the world *toward* the other and is deeply aware that the other has a consciousness of the world that is outside of and beyond one's own. But in a colonial context, the colonized' look does not affect the colonist with a recognition of a different point of view. This negation of recognition between the colonized and colonizers structure social relations and knowledge production.

In a footnote, Fanon introduces the term *lactification* to name one of the possible responses to the antidialectics of colonized space: the person of color's desire to whiten the body and the mind.[5] Lactification is the name given to the desire for intimacy, relationships, marriage, and even having children based on the other person's proximity to whiteness. Lactification speaks to the way that colonialism and antiblack racism have disciplined the inner life of the colonized including their feelings of desire, perceptions of beauty, and who is an ideal person with whom to form a family alliance. This is not to say that all "interracial" relationships are evidence of a colonized mentality, but rather interracial relationships that are based on a desire for whiteness are examples of lactification.

Fanon situates the phenomenon of lactification as particular to the woman of color. He states, "The black woman has only one way open to her and one preoccupation—to whiten the race. The mulato woman wants not only to become white but also to avoid slipping back. What in fact is more illogical than a mulato woman marrying a black man? For you have to understand once and for all that it's a question of saving the race." Fanon's identification of this phenomenon in Martinique can also be recognized occurring in Mexico in the common idiom "*Casate con un güero para mejorar la raza*" ("Marry a light skinned man to improve the lineage"). However, rather than being specifically about women of color's attitudes toward men, it is a mindset that applies across genders. In fact, the phenomenon of ranking intimacies in terms of "improvement" and "slipping back" or "turning back" will be the linchpin in the sedimentation of lactification in the Spanish colonies.

Fanon ascribes a different trajectory to black men and white women because of one aspect of history. He suggests that sexual relationships between black women and white men are structured by the history of white masters raping enslaved black women and so the relationship is fundamentally condemned to violence. However, Fanon sees white women's relationships to black men quite differently; they are not structured by the same hierarchy of sexual violence. He states, "But relations between a white woman and a black man automatically become a romantic affair. It is a gift and not a rape."[6] In Fanon's account, white women, with no mention of their class location, appear as subjugated to white men, too, and thus can recognize black men as an other. Perhaps the assumptions about white bourgeois femininity of Fanon's time made his assessment possible, however recent research has revealed the very different role they had and continue to have in the colonial project.[7] He is correct that white bourgeois women are subordinate to white bourgeois men, but white working-class women are also situated within the triadic schema, and both hold stratified positions above indigenous and black people generally.

An examination of the semiotic structure of the *sistema de castas* provides the means to better understand the way in which working-class white women were situated in the Spanish colonial context, a question that remains unclear in decolonial feminism. It also helps us better understand the logic of lactification and how it became common sense. The texts I focus on are eighteenth-century letters by Pedro Alonso O'Crowley as well as the casta paintings of the same time period. For the most part, these paintings have only been interpreted as the ideological imposition of the Spanish elite, but what they convey about what it means to be human itself in New Spain has not been examined. There is evidence that at least two of the key painters, Miguel Cabrera and Jose de Ibarra, were in fact *castas*, which introduces a new perspective to the interpretation of their paintings and demonstrates that the ontological assumptions implicit to the *sistema* were understood by people outside the immediate members of the European elite.[8]

The line of questioning I pursue in this chapter focuses on identifying the terms in which the human was redefined prior to the declaration of a de jure colorblind society in the Viceroyalty of New Spain post-1821.[9] This method involves identifying the terms one would use to answer the question "*what are you?*" during the formal colonial period in the Viceroyalty of New Spain and then excavating the conditions in which these categories emerged. An analysis of this semiotic structure helps us discern the conditions in which a particular mode of speaking about the human took shape. It also helps to discern the logic of social relations that was established at the time and evaluate if the same logic is still at work today. If so, knowing these parameters will help articulate a plan of action to enact Wynter's dream of redefining the terms in which the human is understood.

Sylvia Wynter refers to "African descended (and Afro-mixed) populations" as the invisibilized third perspective of the triadic schema. It is the specific group of people in the parenthesis that form "the continuum of new categories of humans (i.e., mestizos and mulattos to which their human/subhuman value difference gave rise) . . . [and that were] brought into existence as the foundational basis of modernity." It is this group that makes up the continuum between human, subhuman, and nonhuman that I will focus on in this chapter to illuminate the specific terms they were brought into existence during the time of "Man 1."[10]

The lay English language term "mixed" is often invoked to speak of mestizos and mulattos despite its frustratingly vague and evasive quality. Critics of mixed race studies, for example, have commented on its liberal antiblack tendencies and some examples certainly affirm this criticism.[11] But it cannot be said to be definitive of nor inherent to the field. Rather, the expressions of the *experience* of being mixed race (rather than the fact of mixed lineage) is telling us something important about the world. In Spanish, the academic term for speaking about "mixed race" is "mestizaje" or "mestizos." Both "mixed" and "mestizaje/mestizos" are applied to a wide variety of histories, morphologies, and experiences across the Americas and are used in very different ways across scholarly projects. Early on in this research it was evident that if these terms were intended to help clarify castas' social location and identify the source of their inferiorization they were facing an uphill battle, precisely because of their vague and encompassing qualities. Criticisms that "mixed" peoples, mestizos, and related lexicons of mixedness/mestizaje-as-transcendence actually perpetuate and reinforce antiblack and anti-Indian racism question the suitability of the terms almost as soon as one learns about them. Unlike "Black," "Indian," and "White," categories of the human that at once historicize a person's relationship to the slave master, the settler, and the bourgeoisie and help identify the source of oppression, "mixed" and "mestizo" have been sufficiently appropriated by the criollo elite that they are now too obfuscating to do the work that other racial identifications accomplish. *Mestizo* may work for people who are actually "half Indian/half Spanish," but this is not the precision with which the term is used. Nevertheless, it is the terminology that has reached a level of popularity and so serves as a beginning point for my inquiry.

In this chapter I do not promote reifying the vocabulary of casta or of any particular casta category to supplant "mestizaje" or "mixed race." Rather, I demonstrate that this is a vocabulary we have inherited that was put into practice at the same time as the terms black, Indian, and white and thus speaks to a history and consciousness that must be contended with as part of the coloniality of being. The notion that different kinds of human beings "mix" has been so naturalized that it appears to be operating at a metaphysical level, however, it is a way of thinking about human reproduction and actions that is historically specific.

Despite the common but false perception that "mixed" people themselves are fairly novel creatures due to increasingly relaxed racial attitudes, if we take "mixed" to be the referent for the people who have emerged out of the intimacies of four continents, what *is* novel is the social practices that emerged in relation to these intimacies in the wake of Spanish colonization.[12] Spanish colonialism set precedents for British colonialism and the underlying logic of typologizing people based on morphology can be traced to this period.[13]

What is missing from prevalent narratives of *mestizaje* is a systematic account of the *sistema de castas* that systematized and institutionalized our meaning of "being mixed." If our understanding of race and racism is attentive only to what Wynter identifies as the time of Man 2, then the racial semiotic structures of Man 1 that are crucial for understanding racialization in the Spanish viceroyalties are rendered invisible.[14] The *sistema de castas* that shaped the Space of Otherness for Man 1 in addition to the inscription of the Indian and Black, justified and provided a coherent logic to the new division of labor and property. It also provided basic guidelines for how to fit the proliferation of variously "mixed" people into a socioeconomic system to benefit a very small group of Spanish elite. But where did this notion of "mixed" humans come from? Why are people described in this way? The answer lies in Stoicist and Platonicist influence on Renaissance thinkers on the nature of the human; a legacy we are still contending with today. A close reading of casta paintings depicting specifically Afro-mixed people makes the history of lactification in New Spain apparent. Understanding the scope of the redefinition of the human under colonialism and the philosophical underpinnings of the semiotic structure in which we communicate provides us with specific parameters to assess whether our actions are sufficiently decolonizing the ways in which we understand what it means to be human.

A NOTE ON THE CASTA PAINTERS

As might be expected, one of the founders of the Academy of Art in Mexico City in 1722 was the son of a distinguished family. Juan Rodríguez Juárez, a casta painter himself, was the child of at least four generations of painters who had the financial, social, and political clout to found an institution where "there was a desire on the part of these artists to elevate the status of painting to one of the liberal arts of the viceroyalty, and to demonstrate that it was an intellectual pursuit and not merely a manual craft."[15] What has not been discussed in recent scholarship on the *sistema de castas* is the apparent lineage of other prolific casta painters, two of whom are included in these pages: Miguel Cabrera and José de Ibarra. Miguel Cabrera was believed to be of pure Zapotec Indian lineage, but was accused at one point of being of "color quebrada"—a casta. There are no known vital records to definitively support either conclusion, however there is record of the dispute over his lineage and the fact that he was generally understood to be Zapotec.[16] Jose de Ibarra was himself mulato.[17] What is evident from what little is known of these painters, is that two of the three paintings examined in this chapter were painted by colonial/racial subjects. This places their paintings and institutional building efforts to establish the Academy of Arts in Mexico City in a new light. Casta paintings were not necessarily the exclusive efforts of *peninsular* or *criollo* elite to project dominant ideologies, but also the contemplation of dominant ideologies by indigenous and casta intellectuals who were subject to its racialization. The paintings are arguably limited to the level of description, but they make colonial/racial ideology of New Spain explicit and to that end are invaluable. Similarly, the establishment of the Academy of Arts in Mexico City was not necessarily an attempt of Spanish elites to simply replicate the arts academy in Cadiz as has been normally assumed, but may have also been an effort on the part of colonial/racial subjects to advance themselves as intellectuals, artists, and social beings.

The casta paintings were a genre of painting that *castas* could create without permission and approval in contrast to paintings of religious themes. So, while an explicit critique of the *sistema de castas* may have been dangerous for the casta painters to make, and it is possible they were themselves invested in the system due to lactification, the casta paintings as description, contemplation, reflection, and articulation of what was safe to paint leaves us a rich archive to examine the normative symbolic racial, gender, and sexual codes of New Spain.

THE THEORY OF ANIMAL-HUMAN CONNECTION IN THE SPANISH VICEROYALTY OF NEW SPAIN

> Although vicious men keep the appearance of their human bodies, they are nevertheless changed into beasts as far as the character of their souls is concerned.
>
> —Boethius, 480–524 AD

> *Lobos*, *cambujos*, and *coyotes* are fierce people of bizarre customs.
>
> —Francisco de Ajofrin, 1763

In Plato's *Republic*, Socrates instructs Adeimantus: "We aren't all born alike, but each of us differs somewhat in nature from the others, one being suited to one task, another to another. . . . The result, then, is that plentiful and better-quality goods are more easily produced if each person does one thing for which he is naturally suited."[18] Socrates later continues, "There are other servants, I think, whose minds alone wouldn't qualify them for membership in our society but whose bodies are strong enough for labor."[19] Plato introduced an interesting division between the mind and the body, and between the real and the illusory. For Plato, what we understand through the bodily senses is inconsistent and ever changing and thus fundamentally unknowable. What is true remains so despite what we feel about it and despite social or political climates. For Plato it was only ideas that were real. Ascribing only ideas as real is the premise for introducing a hierarchical divide between the mind and the body. According to Plato, ideas are the realm of the mind and our senses are the realm of the body. Human life was argued to be a rationally ordered existence and this was interpreted to mean that the human ideal required the suppression of sensual life. Below the life of the mind was the life of base instincts and that was, supposedly, most fully represented in the animal world.

In the *Republic*, the relationship between human nature and the division of labor is understood to be important for the effective governance of a city, but also about a relationship between individual temperaments and specific vocations. It was also about occupational stratification and for justifying the notion that everyone had their proper place in society. A person's soul, their individual temperament, and their place in society was symbiotic. However, the transition between the understanding of the soul as a strictly internal phenomenon regarding one's character to the notion that one's soul not only defines one's character, but also one's morphology occurs during the colonization of the Americas. From the sixteenth to eighteenth century, a semiology that correlated one's individual temperament with skin color and hair texture was normalized. The name given to the stratification of labor, souls, and morphology was the *sistema de castas*.

The terms developed to identify particular groups of *castas* in New Spain number in the dozens, but the eighteenth-century colloquial terms to denote individuals of African, indigenous, and European mixture specifically were *pardo* (dark skinned), *lobo* (wolf), *morisco* (derived from "moor," but used to denote lighter skinned people of European and African mix), and *coyote* (American wolf). *Zambo* and *zambaigo* were common in the sixteenth century, but fell out of use by the end of the century.[20] A casta painting by José de Ibarra depicts the child born of a *mestiza* (half Indian/half Spanish) and a *mulato* (half black/half Spanish) as a *Lobo Tente en el Aire*; (Wolf, Hold Yourself in Mid-Air). *Mulato* is a term used to denote a person of half black/half Spanish lineage derived from "mule."[21] Identifying particular humans in zoological terms introduced a semiotics of human/animal relations. It connects the two worlds through stratification. The conclusion that is drawn here is not to rehabilitate Afro-castas to the level of Man, away from animals, but rather to foreground how the relationship between humans and animals was redefined and stigmatized as a specifically racially stratified project under colonialism. It is in relation to not only "black" and "Indian" categories that Spanish colonists articulated a conception of Man as a specific ethno-class of the human, but also in relation to mules, horses, wolves, and coyotes. This is not an attempt to merely add nuance or complicate Sylvia Wynter's triadic schema, but rather to contribute to a fuller understanding of how the triadic schema worked on an everyday level in relation to the millions of people who are identified as neither black nor Indian, but are of those lineages and histories. It addresses the millions of colonial/racial subjects who are neither claimed by an indigenous community nor are visibly identified as black due to their indeterminant "mixture." The articulation of intimacy between

African, Indian, and European as the production of a variety of animal species are crucial to colonial ideology because they explain the relationship between not only black to white and Indian to white, but between Black and Indian also. Reproduction between Black and Indian in any combination was likened to producing new types of beings that were constitutionally more akin to animals than to humans. What will mitigate this relationship is increased contact with Spaniards: the more Spanish ancestry one can acquire for future generations, the more of a gentle constitution one will have. Additionally, the combination of being of lighter skin and having one's family alliance recognized by the church would further cement one's proximity to whiteness. Eighteenth-century marriage records from Mexico City indicate that petitions to marry *moriscos* far outnumbered petitions to marry *lobos*, despite the fact that *lobos* were four times larger in numbers than *moriscos*.[22]

Wolves have been recast in a positive light in contemporary popular culture, but during the Renaissance wolves were referentially used in an entirely pejorative sense. The use of *lobo* and *coyote* as two of the main zoological terms for denoting people of "mixed" black, Indian, and European lineage

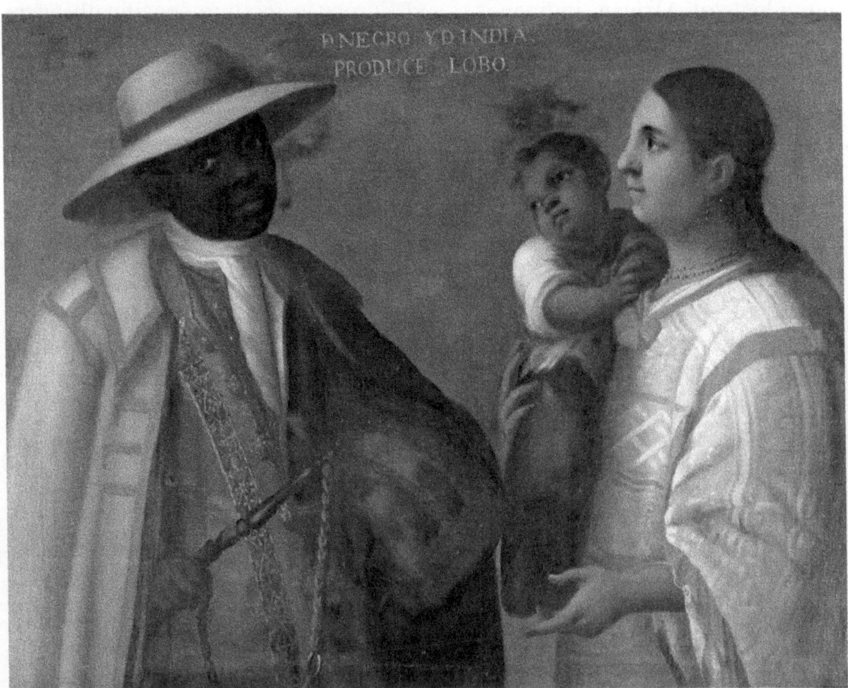

Figure 2.1 Attributed to Juan Rodríguez Juárez, *De negro y India, Produce Lobo* (Black and Indian Produce a Wolf), ca. 1715, oil on canvas, 80.7.9 × 105.4 cm. Breamore House, Hampshire, England.

carries specific meaning. The wolf was the emblematic beast of avarice and cupidity during the Renaissance, and so it provides us with some insight into how racialization was operating at the time. To be called a *lobo* invoked a long history of representing violent, greedy, akratic, hypocritical, and heretical tendencies through the genus *canis*.[23]

The *sistema de castas* was a classification of difference that also provided justification for colonization: in fact, the Spanish were shoring up all resources and were themselves perpetrators of sexual violence.[24] However, classifying the children of "mixed" Black and Indian lineage in animal terms, the Spanish elite could, at the level of perception, project their own avarice onto those most vulnerable in colonial society. Indeed, the offspring of such "mixtures" that crossed Indian, black, and Spanish lines were seen as the

Figure 2.2 Attributed to José de Ibarra, *De mulato y mestiza, lobo tente en el aire* (from Mulatto and Mestiza, Wolf-Hold-Yourself-in-Mid-Air), ca. 1725, oil on canvas, 164 × 91 cm. Museo de América, Madrid.

product of licentious desire and leading to the creation of a morally depraved world. However, this did not mean that the Spanish as the main perpetrators of sexual violence were predetermined as constitutionally licentious or greedy, but rather that they were temporarily misled into sin.[25] Their children must bear the brunt of their actions and be cast as mules, wolves, and coyotes.

Coyote was not a term popular in European symbolic systems, but rather gained popularity in the Spanish viceroyalties. The *coyote* looks similar to the European grey wolf, but is of the Americas. Whereas *lobo* was more commonly used to denote Afro-Indian mixtures, *coyote* was the term to denote people who were of *Mestizo* and *Indio* parentage; someone who was three-fourths Indigenous and one-fourth European was a wolf sub-species unique to the Americas. The animal referents were a clear warning about "slipping back" toward black or Indian. A *mestizo/a* should not bear children with a "pure" Indian person, but rather someone with Spanish lineage. Conversely, a *mulato* should not mix with a black person or a *lobo*, but with another person with closer proximity to the Spanish.

To be recorded as a legitimate birth was to be born to parents married in the Catholic Church, and not surprisingly, the largest group to participate in marriage to the end of the 1700s were Spaniards with other Spaniards. Illegitimate children were thus not necessarily born to single mothers, but could be born to parents or extended family that simply cohabitated without official recognition of the church.[26] Up through the eighteenth century to be a *casta* was synonymous with being illegitimate, for few marriages between *castas* occurred.[27] Thus, to be *casta* for the first three hundred years of Spanish colonization was associated with being a product of licentiousness for even when the child was raised by both parents, living in a sexual union outside of marriage was understood as a sin.

COYOTES, MULES, AND WOLVES: NEW GENRES OF MAN

Coyotes

A comparison of the paintings *De Mestizo y de India, Coyote*, and *De Mestizo y Española; Castizo* exemplify the logic of lactification in the explicitly class/race/sexual terms of the *sistema de castas*. Children born to (likely illegitimate) *mestizos* and plebeian *Indios*, meaning one-quarter Spanish, did not necessarily mean an increase in status, as the name "coyote" given to such children communicates. The vegetables in the bottom left corner of the painting identify the *mestizo* as a food vendor, and thus of the working poor. Food vending was long associated with indigenous women before colonization and remained one of the economic possibilities for them after colonization.[28] The fact that he is a food vendor indicates his family's limited social and economic resources as well as that his life has "slipped back" toward his wife's socioeconomic position.

The mule to the right of the *mestizo* was a symbol of licentiousness, stupidity, stubbornness, and laziness, and even of the devil himself in Renaissance imagery.[29] The mule, as previously mentioned, was the animal from which half black/half Spanish people were associated via the term *mulato*. The mestizo's head is turned toward his partner, but his eyes are cast in the direction of the mule where it is visible in his peripheral vision. The mule is a part of what Frank Wilderson has identified as the long history of "Settler civil society's long-standing commonplace and quotidian phobias inspired by the image—and acoustic—iconography of Blackness as an unspecified and undisputed threat."[30] The painting is a warning against "slipping back" through forging an alliance with an indigenous woman that would situate

Figure 2.3 Miguel Cabrera. *De mestizo y de india, coyote* (from Mestizo and Indian, Coyote), 1763, oil on canvas, 132 × 101 cm. Col. Elisabeth Waldo-Dentzel, Multi Cultural Music and Art Foundation of Northridge, California.

Figure 2.4 Attributed to José de Ibarra, *De Mestizo y española, castizo* (from Mestizo and Spanish woman, castizo), ca. 1725, oil on canvas, 164 × 91 cm. Museo de América, Madrid.

the *mestizo* in closer proximity to blackness. At the same time, the painting invokes the nuanced hierarchy of the *sistema de castas*: his position is approximate to *mulatos* specifically rather than the zero-degree of "pure" blackness, a point that will be examined shortly.

The aggressive, insubordinate nature of the children born to a *mestizo/India* mixture is evident in the child holding up a bar as if about to strike his father on the head. The child displays little respect for his father, and the baby's bare bottom suggests a lack of modesty and signals poverty. The painting portrays the punishment for a half-breed man turning away from the white father writ large: poverty, animals for children, cast toward blackness; nothing short of abjection. The difference between the paintings of a *mestizo* having children with an Indian woman versus that of a *mestizo* having children with a Spanish woman are stark.

When the mestizo turns toward a Spanish woman with whom to form a family alliance, the *mestizo's* social, familial, and economic reality reverses: he and his family are dressed in fine fabrics of Spanish style. The son is walking calmly and appropriately in front of the couple. The composition of the painting communicates orderly progress as they walk talking in a relaxed manner to each other. While there is no direct reference to the *mestizo*'s profession, we can gather that he is in a comfortable situation. The message is clear: colonial/racial subjects are to form alliances with the Spanish if they want a better life. Turn to your indigenous and African side and form family alliances with them and you will suffer the consequences. And this was true for colonized men in New Spain as well as for colonized women. By pursuing a relationship on the basis of the other person's proximity to whiteness, and thus seeking approval in the eyes of the White Father, love as the basis of the relationship has been set aside, sustaining the logic of lactification.[31]

Mules/Mulatos

Mulatos as the point of reference for indicating the bottom levels of degeneracy *among castas* was not only depicted in *casta* paintings, but was also expressed by writers such as Pedro Alonso O'Crowley, a merchant and distinguished member of scientific societies in Europe. O'Crowley wrote a manuscript in 1774 titled *Idea compendiosa del reino de Nueva España.* The original manuscript is housed in the Biblioteca Nacional in Madrid and was translated into English in 1972. In it, O'Crowley attributes the birth of "mixed-bloods" to human weakness and succinctly sketches out the logic of lactification. On *mulatos* he has this to say:

> It is known that neither the *Indio* nor *Negro* contends in dignity and esteem with the Spaniard; nor do any of the others envy the lot of the *Negro*, who is the "most dispirited and despised." Likewise, the basic stocks and their compounds uniformly rate lowest among the mixed-bloods the *mulato*, notwithstanding the characteristic high spirit with which he customarily performs his duties with a gallant air and (even though humbled in service to a Spaniard) at the same time aims to establish his position on a higher level than the rest, in which ambition he has in large part succeeded, especially as regards the Indians, whom he treats as inferiors, using them as servants.[32]

In the lived experience, to be mixed with Spanish, even as a *mulato*, did have benefits over and above "pure" Indians, but this benefit was deeply gendered and limited to half of the *mulato* population in Mexico City.[33] However,

I want to underscore here O'Crowley's reference to *mulatos* as the "lowest among the mixed bloods." He continues:

> To those contaminated with the Negro strain we may give, over-all, the name of *mulatos*, without specifying the degree or the distance direct or indirect from the Negro root or stock, since we have clearly seen, it colors with such efficacy, be it the first union with an Indian or Spaniard or a mixture of these, that it always results in some kind of *mulato* mixture, which even the most effective chemistry cannot purify. Many pass as Spaniards who in their own hearts know they are *mulatos*, and those known to be such are sometimes, more leniently, called *pardos* just as Negroes are sometimes called *morenos*.[34]

It is worth taking note of O'Crowley's choice of words in his description, particularly "stock," "compound," and "mixture." They invoke the words of Plato in his explanation of the person and the soul in *Phaedrus*. Plato's narrative of winged horses and a charioteer is a cornerstone to his philosophy of the relationship between reason, spirit, and appetite. Plato explains that mortals are akin to horses that have lost their wings: "the one that has lost its wings is swept along until it lays hold of something solid, where it settles down, taking on an earthly body, which seems to move itself because of the power of soul, and the whole is called a living creature, soul and body fixed together, and acquires the name 'mortal.'" The soul, in the case of mortals, is a mixture. Of noble and good on the one side, "while the other is the opposite and has the opposite sort of bloodline."[35] In Plato's dialogues there is a significant practice of using animals to explain various phenomena, particularly regarding the human constitution. In other words, there is a classical intellectual tradition of speaking about animals as akin to humans. It is from this context and tradition that a new schema of "mixtures" of people will be theorized in the Spanish colonial semiotics of *castas*. As Wynter explains, intellectuals of Spanish colonization interpreted the relationship between Indigenous and Black peoples as a hierarchy between the acme and nadir of the sub-human.[36] However, *castas* were distinctly situated within this same sub-human status, but could be classified above or below the Indigenous person in the first degodded "descriptive statement" of the human in history. And who was above or below depended on specifics; enslaved Indigenous peoples would be most clearly situated in the Black category, just as their being free, Spanish speaking, and Catholic could situate them in the *casta* category. To complicate this, enslaved Indigenous peoples in the Americas would learn the languages, cultures, and practices of the masters, they could be "mixed" in the same violent ways that enslaved African peoples were, but also not assimilated into the master's ethnoclass.

Wolves

> But the soul which is polluted and engrossed by the corporeal, and has no eye except that of the senses, and is weighed down by the bodily appetites, cannot attain to this abstraction. In her fear of the world below she lingers about the sepulchre, loath to leave the body which she loved, a ghostly apparition, saturated with sense, and therefore visible. At length entering into some animal of a nature congenial to her former life of sensuality or violence, she takes the form of an ass, a wolf or a kite.
>
> —Plato, *Phaedo* 82a

According to Bartolomé de las Casas, the "new world" was neither Christian nor necessarily heretical, but rather naive and ready to be brought into the fold of the Christian family. The Americas as an *atopos* place—the as-yet-to-be-defined, neither here nor there—that Spanish colonists deployed, parallels the concept of place in Book X of Plato's *Republic*.[37]

There are multiple interpretations of Plato's descriptions of transmigration between animals and humans in contemporary scholarship, but none have examined its interpretation vis-á-vis the *sistema de castas*. The *casta* paintings provide an invaluable primary source for examining the "logic of our present order of discourse" as first articulated in the Spanish colonial system. For example, Laurie Shannon's *The Accommodated Animal,* explains the current ways in which "the animal" is dominantly nominalized as without reason emerges from Descartes' seventeenth-century construction of it in *Discourse on Method*. What this chapter demonstrates is that, in the Spanish colonial context, the theory of human/animal *transmigration*, rather than a strict dichotomization, was being elaborated to explain "mixed" people as a continuum between human and animal.

It is worthwhile to note at this point that the *sistema de castas* as practiced in everyday life held more contradictions, irregularities, and fluidities than the paintings suggest. But what we can extrapolate from the paintings is the logic of the semiotic structure, and specifically that Plato's dialogues were influential in providing a vocabulary and theoretical framework for thinking through the constitution of *castas* and their relationship to "pure" blooded people.

Identifying Plato's influence highlights that the whole Western tradition is at issue when decolonization is embraced. The *casta* paintings are pictorial renderings with no written explanations or narratives accompanying them, and with little information regarding their creators, the interpretation of their content is necessarily an exercise in hermeneutics.

"Wolf" and "mule" are the two most commonly used zoological terms used in Mexico City to refer to *Afro-castas*. A survey of the discussion of animals in Plato's works reveal that the wolf is the most disparaged of the animals, and the mule is discussed as the offspring of horses and donkeys. All other animals such as bees, ants, fish, and birds are spoken of in varying degrees of positivity, with the exception of kites and hawks. Dogs, interestingly, are referred to in exceptionally positive terms, and often placed in opposition to wolves. At one point, dogs are used as a metaphor for philosophers, whereas wolves are the Sophists. In *Phaedo*, it states that "tyrants, robbers, and other kinds of unjust people pass in their next lives into the bodies of predators such as hawks, wolves, and kites." Wolves are used to infer the epitome of untrustworthy, dangerous, and threatening behavior.

Horses are probably the most respected and frequently invoked of the animals mentioned; they are described as beautiful, virtuous, and courageous. Donkeys or asses, on the other hand, are gluttons. Their crossbreeding produces the mule, a fact mentioned in *The Statesmen*:

VISITOR: Well, do you want to divide it by the split-hooved and the so-called "single-hooved," or by interbreeding and non-interbreeding? I think you grasp the point.
YOUNG SOCRATES: What's that?
VISITOR: That horses and donkeys are naturally such as to breed from one another.
YOUNG SOCRATES: Yes.
VISITOR: Whereas what is still left of the smooth-headed herd of tame creatures is unmixed in breeding, one with another.
YOUNG SOCRATES: Quite.
VISITOR: So: does the statesman, then, seem to take care of an interbreeding or some non-interbreeding sort?
YOUNG SOCRATES: Clearly, of the non-mixing sort.[38]

It is a brief passage, but it clearly separates animals into two camps: the mixed and the unmixed, and only the non-mixing sort are to receive the State's care. In the colonial context the question that is being consistently raised is over whom do the Spanish have jurisdiction and to what extent? According to Plato, the Statesman has a primary interest in the well-being of "the non-mixed." The relationship between the Statesman and "the mixed" will follow a different set of rules. Plato does not expand on the relationship that the "mixed" will have with the Statesmen, but we can see the influence the intellectual work of Plato had in forging a semiotic code of human difference in the colonial context, particularly given the early establishment of two separate republics for Indigenous peoples and Spanish settlers in New Spain.[39]

COLONIAL INTERPRETATIONS OF PLATO ON THE NATURE OF ANIMALS

> And not only did men pass into animals, but I must also mention that there were animals tame and wild who changed into one another and into corresponding human natures—the good into the gentle and the evil into the savage, in all sorts of combinations.
>
> —Plato, *The Republic*

In a rather fascinating discussion of the relationship between the human and the animal, in Book X of *The Republic*, Plato discusses the fluid transmigration of souls from beast to human and vice versa. The only caveat being that animals were divided into two camps: the gentle and the savage, as were human natures. Not only does the story suspend the division between human and animal worlds, but says that humans can actually become animals, and vice versa.[40]

Proclus, the foremost philosopher of antiquity, argues against the implications of Plato's narrative of transmigration in favor of taking the position that the human soul is impervious to the animal. Plotonius argues that we can say that the human soul is not different in nature or being from an animal based on Plato's myth, but rather what differentiates them is the emphasis on the rational or the intellectual rather than sensation. Ficino turns the myth into a metaphor, arguing that transmigration is an entirely internal phenomenon that speaks to a change in character rather than a literal crossing of souls from human to animal. Contemporary readings question whether we can only understand the myth as an allegory in a more literal interpretation.[41] We will see that Plato's dialogues take on new meaning in the Spanish colonies.

Plato's distinction between gentle and savage animals and the possibility of transmigration with people of parallel human natures, segues well with the Aristotelian debates of the sixteenth century distinguishing "natural slaves" from "man."[42] What Plato's work provided is the needed framework for explaining the "mixing" of natural slaves, nature's children, and man.

Rather than Ficino's rendering of Plato's myth as a purely internal phenomenon, in the colonial encounter a person's morphology becomes the external reflection and manifestation of the soul. The externalization of the so-called savage soul is manifest through the division of labor and the effort of Spanish colonists to monopolize all resources. The naming of Afro-castas as *lobos* and *mulatos* is to identify the transmigration of wolf and mule to human form. There are records that demonstrate that Bartolomé de las Casas and Francisco Cervantes de Salazar (the rector of the Royal and Pontifical University of Mexico founded in 1551) were both familiar with Ficino's commentaries on Plato.[43] The savage (sensory dominated) soul is connected to the natural slave who is visually black. The gentle (rational) soul is Man who is white. The Indian, then can be understood as having an essentially gentle soul so long as they don't give way to lust or avarice, and remain in the company of Man, even if in a subordinate position. The permeability and fluidity of the Indian soul and the White soul in the *sistema de castas* is contrasted with the impermeability and steadfast nature of the black soul. Transmigration does indeed exist, but only between Spaniard and Indian as two animals of "noble and good" disposition. Transmigration between women and men of similar "souls" is also possible, according to Plato. However, the "opposite nature" of the African, man or woman, cannot successfully transmigrate between European and Indian, for they are not of similar character or soul. The social and cultural demands of Spanish colonialism cast African (and Afro-mixed) people as the permanent "outside" of Indian-Spanish relations.

Now back to the question of "mixture." Why does Miguel Cabrera in his painting *De mestizo y India, coyote* signify and Pedro Alonso O'Crowley state that the *mulato* is the point of reference for all Afro-castas, rather than *negro* itself? It brings to sharp focus the specifics of how the triadic schema worked in the face of the proliferation of "mixed" people. *Castas* were plucked out from "pure" blackness or "Indianness" and assorted as distinct types of being that were more constitutionally similar to other *castas* than to their "parent" groups. Mixed and unmixed were two different groups, as Plato stated. Mixture was understood as a process that fundamentally alters a person's constitution and social location. One of the novel interpretations of Plato's dialogues in the colonial context was to divide "pure" bloods into three different fundamental groups and ascribe them different constitutions, and then further separate them from "mixed" bloods and ascribe each of them different constitutions, depending on their proximity to "pure" bloods.

The logic of the *sistema de castas* situates blackness in the background as "the most dispirited and despised," against which not only whiteness can be discerned, but also *casta* existence. The dehumanization of *castas* is at once linked to, but distinguished from blackness. A claim to Spanish lineage mitigates against abject blackness. The point of reference becomes, then, *mulataje*, to which a variety of Afro-*castas* can be subsumed but not necessarily conflated.

An exploration of the terminology "*tente en el aire*" will give us further insight as to why *Afro-castas* were marked off from the category of *negro*.

"MIXED" BLOOD AND THE STOIC INFLUENCE

But if your belief about these things in any way lacked assurance, how from the combining of water, earth, air, and sun came the forms and color of mortal

> things which have now arisen, fitted together by Aphrodite. . . . With earth we perceive earth, with water water, with air divine air, with fire destructive fire, with love love, and strife with baneful strife.
>
> —Empedocles 60(71)–77(109)

The term I want to focus on is one that appeared with some frequency in *casta* paintings, but did not appear to have any colloquial use: *tente en el aire*. The term appears either as a stand-alone category in *casta* paintings or in addition to another, such as *lobo*, that did have colloquial usage. To capture the detail to which the *casta* paintings went to systematize the variety of "mixtures" occurring in the viceregal capital, this (incomplete) description of the *tente en el aire* is offered by historian Kenneth Mills:

> A *tente en el aire*—a localized Mexican expression meaning "suspended in air"—was the offspring of six possible racial mixtures (a *torno-atrás* man and a Spanish woman, a *cambujo* man and an Indian woman, a *salta-atrás* man and an *albarazado* woman, a *jibaro* man and a mulato woman, an *albarazado* man and a *jibaro* woman, or a *cambujo* man and a *calpamulo* woman). Most of these castas themselves were the products of a comparable number of alternative unions. To consider only one of the parents of a *tente en el aire* for the purposes of illustration, a *cambujo* man (derived from the name of a reddish-black stallion) might himself be the offspring of some nine possible parental combinations.[44]

I want to underscore two points from this quote. First, that by the eighteenth century there were already multiple generations of mixed Indigenous/African/European peoples. Second, that to "mix lineages" in eighteenth-century New Spain was understood to produce a new type of species. While these terms, *cambujo*, *jibaro*, *albarazado*, may not have been colloquially common, they do speak to the logic of racialization. To be "mixed" was to be constitutionally distinct from "pure" lineages and thus was distinguished from the parent groups and of a new classification of being. Reports of self-identification in census records signal that people were not only being identified as distinct *castas* of people, but that "mixed" peoples were themselves also identifying in these *casta* terms.[45] Thus, a person of "mixed" black African or "mixed" Indian lineage would not have been identified as "black" or "Indian" in colonial New Spain, but as a distinct type of being.

A reading of Galen's physical theory is necessary to help us understand the meaning of *tente en el aire*, a glossed over and otherwise unclear term in the pictorial rendering of the *sistema de castas*. *Tente en el aire* was used across a wide array of *casta* paintings beyond what Mills describes above, but always mixtures that were beyond the biracial paradigm: those who were Indian, white, *and* black. The ubiquity of the term thus denoted a state of being for those who could not, apparently, be conflated with *mulatos* (black/Spanish), *mestizos* (Indian/Spanish), or *zambos* (black/Indian).

In Renaissance theories of embodiment, the body was porous and susceptible to the environs in which it lived. This meant not only that the body was constituted by its home environment, but that interactions with other people also actively shaped one's constitution. Family alliances, in particular, were crucial for maintaining a certain bodily composition. Sustained interactions between Christians and Muslims, Jews, or Protestants, for example, were thought to negatively change one's temperament, intelligence, and abilities.[46] This logic was then applied to interactions between black African, American Indian, and white European peoples. Up until the colonization of the Americas it was understood that a person could generally rehabilitate their constitution from corruption or illness. However, the language of immutability of the black African lineage set a limit to the transcendent possibilities of the "mixed" human, permanently "staining" one's lineage.

The notion that the environs permeated the body was advanced by Empedocles in the fifth century and would influence Hippocrates and Galen in the following centuries. Medical students in Mexico City studied Galen up until the nineteenth century and his work would have been familiar to formally educated Spaniards in the Spanish viceroyalties.[47] Galen, a first-century Greek philosopher, was very influential for Spanish intellectuals both in Spain and in Spanish viceroyalties from the sixteenth through eighteenth centuries.[48] In the context of Spanish colonialism, Stoicist philosophy took on a new life that provided key vocabulary for talking about the human. Importantly, speaking about people as "mixed" is one of the contributions of the Stoicist intellectual framework and has particular implications for how we have come to conceptualize the limits of coherent human categories.

"Mixing" was the very process of life coming into being. The mixing of the four fundamental elements—earth, air, fire, and water—in varying degrees is what produced the difference between people, trees, and the sun. From four basic roots emerged the plethora of life forms, and in death the beings returned to their root states. Empedocles thought it was through love that the elements came together in, for example, "a mass of mortal limbs," and then through strife that they then "wander, each apart on the shore of life."[49] Mixing was thus the verb of life that manifested the elements in specific types and forms through the dialectics of love and strife. Reading Empodocles explains why the terminology of "mixing" was central to Spanish colonial epistemology that has become the central motif in discussions of the "multiracial" individual or group.

In sharp contrast to Jared Sexton's necessary statement that "there is no interracial sex" as his way to "attack on every front the appearance of biological racism" that seeks to naturalize misanthropic skepticism, Empedocles,

Hippocrates, and Galen all saw the mixing of types of beings as fundamental to the life cycle. Living in a different world before the modern/colonial world system, these philosophers saw all individuals as humoristically distinct, but capable of becoming the ideal happy, healthy person.

The specific constitutions of "men" and "women" were understood to be hierarchical to each other, but linked and transmigratory. In fact, Renaissance theories of embodiment maintained that the human body, both male and female, was potentially fluid and permeable. This theory of embodiment was pressed for more specifics as colonization forced new kinds of encounters in a context of exploitation. Because different environments were understood to produce different types of beings and explained the visible differences between them (e.g., the excess of sun in Africa was understood to produce people with darker skin due to exposure), it was a logical extension to think of people from different environments as fundamentally different types of beings. All matter arose from these four elements but in different proportions of mixture with particular qualities: hot, moist, cold, and dry. In the human body the elements were manifest in the form of humors: blood, black bile, yellow bile, and phlegm. Illness, including poor mental health, was attributed to having an imbalance of the humors that could be rectified by food, drugs, and practices such as bloodletting, vomiting, and sweating. Pursuing the medical history of mixedness and humorology, the term *mestizaje* can be traced to Arabic medical literature and the word *misáj* denoting "health" in Arabic, Persian, and Turkish that influenced Spanish physicians. In Arabic, the etymology of the word *misaj* can be traced to a verb meaning "to mix" in reference to the four elements or properties as well as carrying the meaning of temperament or balancing. It is from this etymology and the influential theories of Galen that we also have the language of "mixed" to speak about the human.[50]

The qualities of air (*tente en el aire*) were hot and moist. It was considered an active element in the same company as fire. Air was what held objects independently from each other. In the Stoic narrative, air was one of the four base elements of all objects in the universe and was understood to have unique and important qualities. The world, including each person, was made of the four elements and balance between them was key to health and happiness. By ascribing people as "hold you in mid-air," or "suspended in air," was to point out the imbalance of their constitution.[51] To be suspended in air was shorthand for a series of "hot" or active qualities ascribed to blackness: predisposition to thievery, idleness, excessive drinking, sexual licentiousness, concubinage, irresponsibility, and so forth. Not only in terms of moral constitution, but physical also. In a unique turn in the history of the philosophy of the body, during the Renaissance the African body's constitution was deemed permanent and immutable and then applied to the logic of the *sistema de castas*. *Castas* were not assumed to be the beginning of a new future of people, but rather they signaled an imbalance in nature that needed to be rectified. The legacy of this semiotic structure is the assertion that a "mixed-race" person is fundamentally inferior, has no future, and must be reined in.

BEING MIXED AS MORAL FAILURE

Stoic philosophy placed great importance on morality as the main terrain in which human beings could effect change in the world. If the conditions in which one was born and the state of the world were out of one's control, what was possible to control was one's psychological state and moral judgment.[52] This basic principle has far reaching implications in a context of exploitation colonialism, Spanish supremacy, and the *sistema de castas*. If Spaniards born in Spain are deemed to be the only representatives of truly balanced human beings, and the emergence of *castas* are the result of licentiousness and poor judgment—that is to say a failed moral compass—then rectifying the imbalance lie internally in making the correct choices and decisions that will restore balance as opposed to challenging the logic of racialization. This is not only for Spaniards who must refrain from causing humoral imbalances through associating with Africans, plebeian Indians, and *castas*, but for *castas* themselves. Social change is rendered as an interior process that manifests in decisions specifically regarding sexuality and the formation of family alliances. For *castas*, as people who are perceived as constitutionally imbalanced, the dominant ideology of the period entails hispanicizing oneself as an effort to find balance. If to be Spanish is equated with being the more superior rendering of the human, then being in the presence of Spaniards, speaking Spanish, practicing Spanish Catholicism, wearing Spanish clothing, and so forth, is understood as restoring balance. Crucially, intimacy, sexuality, and bearing children is oriented toward a Spanish ideal through the logic of the *sistema de castas*. Spanish supremacy was an ideology rooted in ancient philosophies of embodiment and health care of the time, but transformed through the colonial project.

"MAN" IS WHITE

None of the *casta* paintings speak of becoming "Negro" or "Indio" again after "mixing." Pedro Alonso O'Crowley does state that after three generations of mixing with Indians, so long as no African lineage is present, the person can return to being an Indian, but this is not represented in the *casta* paintings.[53]

Regardless, the logic of the *sistema de castas* was oriented entirely "upward" toward Spaniards and the whitening of people in the Spanish viceroyalty. It provided a specific trajectory for people to preferably marry white, but at least as light as possible, and to avoid people with black African lineage. However, if one "slipped back," the terminology used was "*torna atras*," "*tente en el aire*," or "*no te entiendo.*"

The Spanish colonial theory of the body was that the African lineage had strong properties, stronger than European ones, and would resurface or overtake the properties of other lineages if mixed. For example, the *casta* category "*torna atras* (turn back)" was to signal that even if the person's African lineage was from a distant generation, a child born to a couple that otherwise looked white could appear with black African features. This was not the case for indigenous mixtures: indigenous lineage was seen as having weaker properties that could be surpassed by the European lineage and thus eventually completely diluted out of a person's constitution.[54]

No amount of "mixing" between black Africans and Europeans would allow acceptance to Spanish elite circles, but the possibility of eventually *passing* as a Spaniard was still, at least theoretically, a window of opportunity. The notion of *calidad* and *clase* were an important aspect of the *sistema de castas* that referred to the way in which one spoke Spanish, their mannerisms, whether or not they attended the Catholic Church, were married in the church, and so forth. It in fact extended the Stoic philosophical position that a person's constitution could be transformed through exposure and/or immersion in a new milieux.

An escape from poverty and dehumanization could be attained by future generations, theoretically speaking, through carefully selected reproduction, the attainment of certain skills, the chance access to capital, and cultural performance. The ideology of the *sistema de castas* proffered a limited kind of freedom to the colonized that need not be fought for nor demanded, that did not threaten Spanish power or wealth, and all that was needed was the right individual choices and perhaps a little luck. The *sistema de castas* was a system of social control through and through.

The *sistema de castas* produced a particular way of thinking about the other in the colonial context that ascribed a person's qualities, characteristics, and capacities based on their visible race and ascribed gender and organized the division of labor based on these differences. A new *logic* to human relations was introduced: from dark skinned to light skinned became a hierarchical typology that meant from savage to civilized, from condemned to godlike, from promiscuous to chaste, from incapable of reason to intelligent, from poor to rich. Additionally and crucially, changing the world was rendered an entirely individual internal process.

THE FORMATION OF THE LACTIFIED SUBJECT IN THE *SISTEMA DE CASTAS*

"Mixed" blood or "mixed" race is a linguistic inheritance that has crossed colonial empires in addition to "Black," "Indian," and "White." It is interesting and crucial to note that over the last five hundred years consistently used terms emerged for three "types" of being *across* colonial empires in the Americas: Negro/black, Indio/Indian, and Blanco/white. However, no consistent term has emerged for the thousands, now millions of "mixed" people who have existed for just as long a period, except for the term "mixed" itself.[55] While there are some terms that gained prevalence in some areas of the Spanish viceroyalties, such as *mestizo*, *castizo*, *mulato*, *morisco*, *zambo*, *cholo*, *lobo*, *coyote*, and *chino*, these were not consistently applied within a colonial empire, and certainly not across colonial empires.[56] The lack of consistent terminology for "mixed" people across empires beyond the adjective signals the work that needs to be done to successfully conduct a transcolonial analysis that is attendant to the triadic model, particularly when not familiar with how different empires racialized "mixed" populations.[57]

Within the triad, the proliferation of "mixed" peoples presented certain challenges to the coherence and reliability of the system that was ideologically solved by the notion that through three generations of Indian miscegenation with Spaniards one could ascend to a membership with the elite. Indian "blood" could surpass Spanish "blood," but black African "blood" remained a permanent stain in one's genealogy. No amount of miscegenation between black Africans and Europeans would allow acceptance to full Christian or Spanish status, and dark skin would return in future generations as can be seen in the *casta* painting, "*De espanol y morisca, produce albino*." This painting presents an opportunity to unpack the casta's subject formation in the colonial context which will give us further insight on the operating logic in the redefinition of the human under Spanish colonialism.

De Espanol y morisca, produce albino is unique in the way the eyes of the woman are positioned. It is the only painting in which her eyes are averted away from the man and child nor focused on a specific task. The eyes through which we are positioned to look at the painting is that of the Spanish man in a deep red velvet coat with golden buttons and silk necktie. He is pointing ahead, appearing to tell her the direction they are to go. The woman, his wife, is dressed in modest but good quality fabrics. The dress is hoisted up to expose her breast, at which a baby with white-blond hair suckles. They appear to be outside walking past the pillar of a large building. In the top right corner the words, "*De español y morisca produce albino*" are written. The woman's slightly furrowed brow as she looks down and away from her

Figure 2.5 Attributed to Juan Rodríguez Juárez, *De español y morisca, produce albino* (Spaniard and Morisca Produce an Albino), ca. 1715.

husband suggests a sense of concern or misgiving. Perhaps she disagrees with the direction he wants to go, or has a concern about the destination. Her misgiving must be read as a metaphor within the context of the sets of *casta* paintings.

The name *morisca/o* was generally used to denote a light-skinned Afro-mixed person, usually of three-quarters Spanish lineage and one-quarter African in New Spain.[58] The painting can be read as conveying a subtle, but clear message given the meaning attributed to a connection between blood, breast milk, and lineage in the eighteenth century: the lineage that "hides" in her blood is being passed on, not only through birth, but through breastfeeding and care. The centrality of the act of breastfeeding foregrounds the connection between mother and child, not only in forming an emotional bond, but how the transmission of bodily fluids gives life to the baby. Breast milk and blood were closely associated in Stoic accounts for the way in which they were understood to transmit both biological and normative traits to future generations.[59] As Maria Elena Martínez has explained, breast milk became one of the main metaphors of cultural and biological contagion, placing particular focus and emphasis on the impurity of women, rather than men, in the Spanish viceroyalties.[60]

The painting foregrounds the race/gender intersection of power relations in New Spain, elucidating how the Spanish encounter with the *casta* is not a reciprocal exchange in a colonial context. The look between two people takes on special importance in Jean Paul Sartre's philosophy; it is the basis of intersubjectivity.[61] Rather, the encounter between Spaniard and *casta* fundamentally places the humanity of the *casta* in question and maintains a subject/object relationship between the two. Racism circumvents the possibility of subject/subject relations across the colonial divide, depicted clearly by the fact that the Spaniard's look is what matters in this image, not the return of her look which would indicate reciprocity. The Spaniard is presented as neutral, without judgment, perhaps even being victimized by the deception of his wife regarding her lineage. If he is aware of her lineage, then it is his foolishness that is shameful and being warned against.

The person becomes a *morisca* through the look of the Spaniard. Regardless of how she may think of herself or the complexity of who she is (her intellect, her goals, her commitments, etc.) the *casta* painting foregrounds an aspect of her facticity at the expense of all others. Who she is is not merely the function of her own actions and projects, but is also a matter of "being-for-others." In this case, being-for-others is in a context of deeply unequal relations. Her fair appearance, as if Spanish, introduces a struggle into her existence that is not the same as *being* Spanish in the colony. She can deny her history and kinship ties and live a life patrolling her words and actions as an attempt to become a part of the Spanish elite. This would make her duplicitous and a liar as O'Crowley noted: in their hearts they know they are mulatos.[62] Otherwise, her life is defined by a history and lineage that is not readily apparent, not inscribed on the visible body, but nevertheless there. Through the look of the Spaniard, she becomes aware of being an object for him and the third-person perspective of herself is revealed: she is locked in a state of objecthood. The experience of feeling shame in this painting highlights the moment at which racist ideology ceases to merely be a Spaniard's opinion about her and instead becomes a mode of her being that is internalized. The painting illustrates the moment at which her "I" is constituted in a colonial context and it is defined by a form of shame, which is to say, a distressed humiliation at the consciousness of being something wrong. Her physical body is the source of her concern or misgiving. Having a baby takes on another meaning in the colonial context that goes beyond the reproduction of the species or a manifestation of love. To have a child now carries the weight of bringing a person into the world that does not improve the husband's lineage and further compounds her shame. The effectiveness of the *sistema de casta* depends on the internationalization and naturalization of shame as attendant to the *casta* body. Subverting shame and not apologizing for one's body or history then becomes an aspect of decolonizing *casta* psychology, which involves taking the struggle into the social world. As Jennifer Lisa Vest has stated, "While validating the fears of others, she can also insist upon refusing to claim the shame as her own."[63]

Transcendence and freedom were harnessed and presented in a unique form in the *casta* paintings: through carefully selected procreation, the child's attainment of certain skills, the chance access to capital, and a carefully curated cultural performance, one's progeny could be free of stigma, that is white. The sequence of paintings reinforces the nuclear family as the frame of reference in which to find one's understanding of self, always in relation to other nuclear families. The family becomes the place in which transcendence can be manifest, thus placing an importance on the heteronormative relationship that goes beyond the formation of alliance for the circulation of wealth. One's very flesh becomes a repository of symbolic wealth with real material implications. Whiteness is linked to material wealth and thus becomes interchangeably desired as the color of stability and well-being.

Freedom from poverty and dehumanization could be attained by future generations, theoretically speaking, through carefully selected reproduction, the attainment of certain skills, the chance access to capital, and/or cultural performance.

The *sistema de castas* produced a particular way of thinking about the self and other in the colonial context that ossified embodiment and applied novel values to morphology, introducing a new logic to human relations. To this day we can hear the haunting of the *sistema de castas* in the idiom "*casate con un güero para mejorar la raza*" (marry a light-skinned man to improve the lineage) or the treatment of children based on their skin tone. Thus, collectively organizing to reject the interaction between heteronormative colorism and economic opportunities is important to the decolonial process.

There are three further lessons we can take from this exposition toward decolonizing the logic of our current order of discourse. First, the notion that people of "pure" lineage are "mixing" when coming into close contact is a specific inheritance from Spanish colonial interpretations of Plato and Stoic philosophy on the metaphysics of being. This took a visual form that ascribed new meanings to phenotype, clothing, and other visible markers. This colonial legacy has become so naturalized that it is operating as a sedimented structure of human relations in the Americas.

Second, shame about "being mixed" is part of the semiotic structure of lactification. A key component of maintaining lactification is to internalize the sense of shame that characterizes being mixed as a pathological struggle of the confused, lost, or tragic mixed breed that can only be rectified by a negation of blackness.

Third, a unique redefinition of human/animal transmigration is elaborated in and through the *sistema de castas*. Not only were black, Indian, and white categories of being produced under colonialism, but also a fourth category, *castas*.

Fourth, in an effort to decolonize the coloniality of being the question needs to be asked if there is another way to think about human relationships across difference besides as "mixing." This question will be taken up more specifically in chapter 4. Thus far, "racial mixing" is a colonial construct used to institutionalize lactification.

Bad faith involves treating one's life as a ready-made world where one has no choice or as if one's choices and actions can instantaneously supercede all structural barriers. The colonial world demands that change be a strictly internal process, and, furthermore, that the only possibility for the colonized is to be white. To take a position in bad faith would be to assume the role of an object in the world and refuse to accept responsibility, however constrained or limited, of making a judgment and taking an action regarding our circumstances. Taking responsibility involves assessing our history, examining the semiotic structures in which we live, and affecting change on a social and structural level. Yet, colonized people are often confronted with the demand to identify ourselves in terms that affirm racial identity as defined by a set of mind independent properties. We will turn to this theme now to further assess how to best push the decolonial turn.

NOTES

1. Michel Foucault, *The Order of Things: An Archaeology of the Human Sciences* (New York: Vintage Books, 1970).
2. Charles Wm. Ephraim, *The Pathology of Eurocentrism: The Burden and Responsibilities of Being Black* (Trenton, NJ: Africa World Press Inc., 2003).
3. Linda Martin Alcoff, "Phenomenology of Racial Embodiment," in *Visible Identities: Race, Gender, and the Self* (Oxford: Oxford University Press, 2006), 194.
4. Frantz Fanon, *Black Skin, White Masks* (New York: Grove Press, 2008), 89.
5. Frantz Fanon, *Black Skin, White Masks* (New York: Grove Press, 1967), 28.
6. Ibid.
7. Thavolia Glymph, *Out of the House of Bondage: The Transformation of the Plantation Household* (Cambridge: Cambridge University Press, 2008); Charletta Suduth et al., *The Maid Narratives: Black Domestics and White Families in the Jim Crow South* (Baton Rouge: LSU Press, 2012).
8. Xavier Moyssen, "La primera academia de pintura en Mexico," in *Anales del Instituto de Investigaciones Esteticas* IX, no. 34 (1965): 15–30; Guillermo Tovar de Teresa, *Miguel Cabrera: Drawing Room Painter of the Heavenly Queen*, 34–36.
9. In 1822, a ban on the use of *casta* categories in legal records was introduced. See Magali M. Carrera, *Imagining Identity in New Spain: Race, Lineage and the Colonial Body in Portraiture and Casta Paintings* (Austin: The University of Texas Press, 2003), 137.
10. Wynter, *Unsettling*, 288 and 309–10.

11. See Jared Sexton, *Amalgamation Schemes: Antiblackness and the Critique of Multiracialism* (Minneapolis: University of Minnesota Press, 2008).

12. Following Lisa Lowe's definition of intimacy: "First, I mean intimacy as spatial proximity or adjacent connection, and with 'the intimacies of four continents' I hope to evoke the political economic logics through which men and women from Africa and Asia were forcibly transported to the Americas, who with native, mixed, and creole peoples constituted slave societies, the profits of which gave rise to bourgeois republican states in Europe and North America. . . . The second meaning . . . is the more common one of privacy, often figured as conjugal and familial relations in the bourgeois home, distinguished from the public realm of work, society, and politics. . . . Finally, there is a third meaning of intimacies in the constellation to be elaborated. This is the sense of intimacies embodied in the variety of contacts among slaves, indentured persons, and mixed-blood free peoples living together on the islands that resulted in "the collision of European, African, and Asian components within the [Caribbean] Plantation, that could give rise to rebellions against the plantation structure itself." Lisa Lowe, "The Intimacies of Four Continents," *Haunted by Empire: Geographies of Intimacy in North American History* (Durham, NC: Duke University Press, 2006).

13. Kate Lowe, "Introduction: The Black African Presence in Renaissance Europe," in *Black Africans in Renaissance Europe*, ed. T. F. Earle and K. J. P. Lowe (Cambridge: Cambridge University Press, 2010), 9–10.

14. Walter Mignolo, who states we need to examine the renaissance.

15. Ilona Katzew, *Casta Painting: Images of Race in Eighteenth-Century Mexico* (New Haven, CT: Yale University Press, 2005), 16.

16. Xavier Moyssén, "La primera academia de pintura en Mexico," *Anales del Instituto de Investigaciones Esteticas* IX, no. 34 (1965): 15–30.

17. Guillermo Tovar de Teresa, *Miguel Cabrera: Drawing Room Painter of the Heavenly Queen*, 34–36. Also, Xavier Moyssén.

18. Plato, *Republic*, 370.

19. Ibid., 371e.

20. See Ben Vinson III, "Moriscos y lobos en Nueva Espana," in *Debates Historicos contemporaneos: Africanos y Afrodescendientes en Mexico y Centroamérica*, ed. María Elisa Velásquez (Mexico DF: Centro de Estudios de Mexicanos y Centroamericanos, 2011), 159–78.

21. Although "mulato" is clearly a Spanish imposition, by the eighteenth century, people were self-identifying with these categories. See Patricia Seed, "Social Dimensions of Race: Mexico City, 1753," *The Hispanic American Historical Review* 62 (1982): 569–606.

22. Vinson III, *Moriscos y lobos*, 5.

23. See Simona Cohen, *Animals as Disguised Symbols in Renaissance Art* (Leiden: Brill, 2008), 179, 209–11.

24. Antonia Castañeda, "Sexual Violence in the Politics and Policies of Conquest Amerindian Women and the Spanish Conquest of Alta California," in *Sexual Violence in Conflict Zones: From the Ancient World to the Era of Human Rights*, ed. Elizabeth D. Heineman (Philadelphia: University of Pennsylvania Press, 2011), 39–55; Deborah A. Miranda, "Extermination of the Joyas: Gendercide in Spanish California," *GLQ*

16, no. 1–2 (2010): 253–284; Zeb Tortorici, "Sexual Violence, Predatory Masculinity, and Medical Testimony in New Spain," *OSIRIS* 30 (2015): 272–294.

25. See chapter 3 of this book for a discussion of colonial sexual violence.

26. Seed, "Social Dimensions," 569–606.

27. Patricia Seed, *To Love, Honor, and Obey in Colonial Mexico: Conflicts over Marriage Choice, 1574–1821* (Palo Alto, CA: Stanford University Press, 1988).

28. Seed, "Social Dimensions," 587.

29. Cohen, *Animals as Disguised a Symbols in Renaissance Art*, 219, 221, and 231.

30. Frank B. Wilderson III, *Red, White, and Black: Cinema and the Structure of U.S. Antagonisms* (Durham, NC: Duke University Press, 2010), 151.

31. I am using the concept of "love" here in the sense put forth by Nelson Maldonado-Torres and Chela Sandoval. Love as a form of agency defined in ethical terms; relationships, in this sense, do not refer to blood relations or alliances (in the Foucauldian sense), but rather the primacy of intersubjective contact: "The demands of a consistent struggle for nonsexist human fraternity, perhaps better put as affiliation (defined by Sandoval as "attraction, combination, and relation carved out of and in spite of difference"), points to the need for a suspension of the ultimate value of the affirmation of identity and to the need of altericity."

32. Pedro Alonso O'Crowley, *A Description of the Kingdom of New Spain*, trans. and ed. Sean Galvin (San Francisco: John Howell Books, 1972), 20.

33. Patricia Seed, "Social Dimensions of Race: Mexico City, 1753," *The Hispanic American Historical Review* Vol. 62, no. 4 (November 1982): 569–606.

34. Pedro Alonso O'Crowley, *A Description of the Kingdom of New Spain*, trans. and ed. Sean Galvin (San Francisco: John Howell Books, 1972), 20.

35. Plato, *Phaedrus*, 246b, trans. Cooper (1997).

36. Sylvia Wynter, "Unsettling the Coloniality of Being/Power/Truth/Freedom Toward the Human, After Man, Its Overrepresentation—An Argument," *CR: The New Centennial Review* 3, no. 3 (2003): 265–266.

37. Plato, "The Republic," in *Complete Works*, ed. John M. Cooper (Indianapolis: Hackett Publishing Company, 1977), 614b–621d.

38. Plato, *Statesman*, 306e, trans. Rowe (1997).

39. Maria Elena Martinez, *Genealogical Fictions: Limpieza de Sangre, Religion, and Gender in Colonial Mexico* (Palo Alto, CA: Stanford University Press, 2008).

40. Plato, *The Republic*, 620a–d.

41. See Francisco J. Gonzalez, "Of Beasts and Heroes: The Promiscuity of Humans and Animals in the Myth of Er," in *Plato's Animals: Gadflies, Horses, Swans, and Other Philosophical Beasts*, ed. Jeremy Bell and Michael Naas (Bloomington: Indiana University Press, 2015), 225–45.

42. Anthony Pagden, *The Fall of Natural Man* (New York: Cambridge University Press, 1982).

43. Susan Byrne, *Ficino in Spain* (Toronto: University of Toronto Press, 2015), 76.

44. Kenneth B. Mills, William B. Taylor, and Sandra Lauderdale Graham, eds., *Colonial Latin America: A Documentary History* (Lanham, MD: Rowman & Littlefield, 2002), 364.

45. R. Douglas Cope, *The Limits of Racial Domination: Plebeian Society in Colonial Mexico City, 1660–1720* (Madison: University of Wisconsin Press, 1995).

46. María Elena Martínez, *Genealogical Fictions: Limpieza de Sangre, Religion, and Gender in Colonial Mexico* (Palo Alto, CA: Stanford University Press, 2008), 54.

47. Sharon Bailey Galsco, *Constructing Mexico City: Colonial Conflicts over Culture, Space, and Authority* (New York: Palgrave Macmillan, 2010), 61.

48. Martinez, *Genealogical Fictions*, 139, 154.

49. Empedocles, *Physics* 26 (20).

50. E. G. Browne, *Arabian Medicine: The FitzPatrick Lectures Delivered at the College of Physicians in November 1919 and November 1920* (Cambridge: Cambridge University Press, 2011), 119.

51. There is a section in Aristotle that also provides some insight. He writes, "We say that a thing is in the world, in the sense of in place, because it is in the air, and the air is in the world; and when we say it is in the air, we do not mean it is in every part of the air, but that it is in the air because of the outer surface of the air which surrounds it. . . . When what surrounds, then, is not separate from the thing, but is in continuity with it, the thing is said to be in what surrounds it, not in the sense of in place, but as part in a whole . . ." *The Basic Works of Aristotle* (New York: The Modern Library, 1941), 275–76. "Tente en el aire" might also then be referring to the specific environs of castas in the Americas.

52. *The Stoic Reader*.

53. O'Crowley, *Description*, 20.

54. Martinez, *Genealogical Fictions*, 154.

55. Seed, "Social Dimensions," Cope, *Limits*. Arguably, the term "mestizaje" is used as a translation of "mixed" and vice versa, despite the historically specific context in which the term "mestizo/a" was used.

56. See Magnus Morner, *Race Mixture in the History of Latin America* (Boston: Little, Brown, and Co., 1967).

57. I use the term "transcolonial" in the following sense: "to underscore that the delineated boundaries of influence by colonial empires were not as fixed as one might believe, and to highlight spaces in which knowing of a confluence of colonialisms is necessary for achieving the goal of intersubjectivity." Daphne Taylor-García, "Decolonial Historiography: Thinking about Land and Race in a Transcolonial Context," *InTensions Journal* Issue 6 (Fall/Winter 2012).

58. Martinez, *Genealogical Fictions*, 56.

59. Galen, *On Semen*, trans. Philip De Lacy (Berlin: Akademie Verlag GmbH, 1992); Galen, *On The Elements According to Hippocrates*, trans. Philip De Lacy (Berlin: Akademie Verlag GmbH, 1996), 139, 141, 145.

60. Martinez, Maria Elena, *Genealogical Fictions: Limpieza de Sangre, Religion, and Gender in Colonial Mexico* (Palo Alto, CA: Stanford University Press, 2011), 56.

61. The look is not solely meant in the literal ocular sense in Sartre; it is fundamentally about a reciprocal exchange and recognition between the self and other.

62. O'Crowley, *Description*, 21.

63. Jennifer Lisa Vest, "The Internally Globalized Body as Instigator: Crossing Borders, Crossing Races," in *Florida without Borders: Women at the Intersections of the Local and Global*, ed. Sharon Kay Masters et al. (Newcastle upon Tyne: Cambridge Scholars Publishing, 2008), 85.

Chapter 3

The Semiotics of Continental Ontologies in Renaissance/ Colonial Knowledge Production

This chapter is, on a broad level, about perception, language, and meaning. It is to understand how language and actions come together to produce and define the terms in which we are hailed, in which we come to understand ourselves and thus, the objects of our knowledge (such as dominant anthropological understandings of the human, as well as the terms under which we organize as collectives). If we take our definition of the human to be a relationship, an examination of colonialism immediately reveals the constant effort on the part of colonists to destroy that and instead posit certain humans as stereotypes. Implicit to the terms we use to refer to human difference in the modern/colonial/capitalist world-system, such as man, woman, white, and black, is an exercise of power that has been deployed to thwart the fundamental relationality of a humane world. One of the terms under which the damnés are hailed to organize in contemporary social movements is *women* and continentally delineated races.

Bear in mind that one of the priority groups who are granted public housing as mentioned in chapter 1, for example, are people escaping abusive relationships. Because women experience a disproportionate level of domestic violence, unequal gendered power relations are a central feature of the preconditions for the damnés in public housing neighborhoods. On the one hand, you bear witness to the violence that some men exact on women simply for being women. On the other, you also know many men of the damnés who are stereotyped as violent, are in fact responsive and responsible people. Furthermore, women of the damnés are also cast as aggressive and violent; the feminine mystique evades us in fundamental ways. You bear witness to the subjugation of all genders of the damnés by employers, housing managers, government officials, and the police. There is a dissonance then, when one enters a discussion of feminism that is premised on a Manichean division between all men and all women. Simone de Beauvoir begins her exposition of gendered existence from the premise, "If I wish to define myself, I first have to say: 'I am a woman'; on this truth must be based all further discussion."[1] But the struggle of women of the damnés is precisely that the same statement is not possible. It must be qualified by race and the colonial context.

Simone de Beauvoir's treatise on gendered existence juxtaposes the opposition between black and white people as parallel to the opposition between men and women.[2] It is a strange juxtaposition because it elides the specificity of gendered relationships between people of color—an elision I argue is fundamental to the way that gender is deployed in the colonial world. Beauvoir's analysis is also couched in a particular class location. Consider this central theme of her book: "The son will be a chief, a leader of men, a soldier, a creator; he will impose his will on the face of the earth, and his mother will share in his immortality; the houses she did not build, the countries she did not explore, the books she did not read, he will give to her. Through him she will possess the world: but on condition that she possesses her son." Clearly, this assessment of gendered relations does not account for the long history of racial capitalism, slavery, and the chronic unemployment or incarceration the damnés have faced.[3] Given these kinds of elisions in twentieth-century feminist analysis, what are the terms under which it is possible to examine the lived experience of women of the damnés? It raises the question, is the category of *woman* as it has been dominantly defined sufficient for examining the power relations affecting colonial/racial subjects? Rather than "mistake the map for the territory" and simply redeploy the terms and descriptions belonging to semiotic structures that affirm a division between all men and women without acknowledging the structure of coloniality, the task here is to provide an account of the cultural systems that better explains the category of *woman* in the colonial context. This is a different project than elucidating the unique situations of particular groups of women of the damnés, or of claiming the category of woman and demonstrating how colonized/racialized men have colluded with colonial agents. It is rather a contribution to contextualizing the category of "women" itself and thus is guided by questions such as, What were the conditions under which gender entered the colonial lexicon? What characteristics were attributed to those deemed women in the colonies and what did they mean? Thus, what does it mean to be cast as a woman in the colonies? This chapter is toward the effort of coming to a working definition of gender that addresses the colonial difference. It reveals that the social and cultural transformations of Renaissance Europe, particularly in terms of knowledge production, had an important role in shaping the semiotics of gender in terms of continental differences in the colonization of the Americas, the slave trade in Africa, and (at that time) trade in India.

What emerges through an analysis of early sixteenth-century representations of "women in the Americas," was that they were used to form the misguided understanding of ontological, stratified, differences between "Europeans," "Indians," "Africans," and "Asians." To be clear, this analysis is at the level of ontology (what exists and how we come to know what exists) and metageography. The naturalization of continental ontologies belies the fact that groups of people can have distinct histories, languages, and cultural practices and not be considered ontologically distinct. In other words, discrete histories and experiences of colonialism and slavery do not have to equate to the social construction of *racial* differences and this has been demonstrated by various studies in comparative slave systems and colonial/imperial practices over the course of human history.[4] It is precisely the fact that an attitude of misanthropic skepticism emerged as a discourse of continental ontology during the colonization of the Americas that decolonial philosophers have pointed to as unique to the modern/colonial/capitalist world-system.

A central premise of the analysis used in this chapter is that meaning is relational. How this is defined in this context is that narratives regarding "Indians" were constituted in relation with other narratives, not only those about "Europeans," but also about "Africans" and "East Indians." The theoretical genealogy of this approach can be traced to semiotics and phenomenology. In the *Course on General Linguistics*, Ferdinand de Saussure makes the argument that words gain their meaning not because the word itself emanates a fundamental connection to the object referred (that relationship is arbitrary), but because a given word sits in contrast within a set of other words. For example, the colors red, white, and black gain their meaning in contrast to one another—specifically, white is understood as not black and not red, black is understood as not red and not white, and so forth. Implicit to understanding what a given word means is in and through the whole network of relationships that words have with each other. The relational character of producing meaning does not stop between signifiers but extends to all objects generally. All objects in the world gain their coherency in relation to other objects. The ways in which we delineate the difference between one object and another is an act of mediation. This is a definitive theme in phenomenological studies.[5]

Let us be clear that the period in which the texts I am examining in this chapter is at a moment in history where the idiom of continents did not yet exist in the way they do now. There was an ongoing debate about land and water masses between different classical theories, but none specified the continental schema we now often take for granted.[6] It was a time when "Europe" was on the economic periphery of Muslim kingdoms and Chinese empires.[7] In fact, it was only the wealth reaped from the colonization of the Americas and the Atlantic slave trade that facilitated Europe's ascension in the global economy.[8]

What, if any, is the relationship between individual perceptions, such as those held by Spanish colonists about the gender and sexuality of the peoples they encountered in the Americas, India, and Africa, and a representational system of contemporary stereotypes? How did the notions about "cannibals," "Amazons," and sexual licentiousness that were so prevalent at the time become an *integrated* part of European cultural perspectives of the "new world" that produce the coloniality of being? An examination of colonial narratives printed in book form provides the opportunity to see the circulation of systems of representation that then inspired writers, visual artists, and playwrights, including William Shakespeare.

It so happens that the book, as it emerged as a collection of bound papers mechanically reproduced with words printed in ink, shares a historical temporality with colonization. When Portuguese explorers were embarking on the first voyages to southern Africa in the early 1440s, Johann Gutenberg, a German goldsmith, among others, were busily working to perfect the reproduction of printed material by mechanical means.[9]

The first book to be mechanically reproduced, the famous Gutenberg Bible, was published in 1452, eleven years after the first voyage by Antam Gonçalves to western Africa with the direct purpose of engaging in a slave raid.[10] The Portuguese slave raids during the forty years prior to Columbus' first voyage across the Atlantic set an important precedent for the kinds of relations that would be institutionalized in the Americas. News from returning slave raiders, and the imaginations it sparked made for remarkable storytelling. The print machine would facilitate both the production of Eurocentric imaginings of "the Americas, Africa and the Orient," feeding colonists with myths of monsters and cannibals, but also used to print the religious texts needed for converting the peoples of the Americas to Christianity.[11] The seemingly contradictory practices for using the printing press in the colonial project would be a hallmark of the technology.

The emergence of the book and the publication of popular texts such as the one focused on in this chapter, *Paesi Nouamente Retrovati*, aided I argue, in the creation of a small but influential imagined community of "civilized, light-skinned, sexually chaste, Christians"—merchants, doctors, scholars, and priests—long before the nationalisms of later centuries that Benedict Anderson discusses in his book *Imagined Communities*.[12]

It is important to note that literacy rates at the beginning of the sixteenth century in Europe were quite low, as only a thin-stratum in Europe were educated to read and write. However, to state that the lower classes were unaffected by the printed word at this time would be inaccurate. Not only would they be influenced by the decisions of the elite, who themselves were informed by what they read, but there were also traveling raconteurs who stood in markets and read from books as a means of making a living.

Although it is obvious that only a small portion of society had direct access to a book like *Paesi Nouamente Retrovati*, its impact on the broader European populace is also germane given how bourgeois ideas/narratives propagate and circulate popularly.

PAESI NOUAMENTE RETROVATI (1507)—COUNTRIES NEWLY DISCOVERED

Paesi Nouamente Retrovati was a collection of so-called discovery letters first published in the northern Italian city of Vicenza in 1507, the same year that *Cosmographiae Introductio* was printed to accompany Martin Waldseemüller's world map *Universalis Cosmographia*. It was published fourteen years after Pope Alexander VI issued a papal bull granting the Spanish crown sovereignty over all lands in the Atlantic inhabited by non-Christians and four years after the establishment of the encomienda system. *Paesi* is an example of "the *distribution* of geopolitical awareness into aesthetic, scholarly, economic, sociological, historical, and philological texts" with which European culture will forge its identity as ontologically distinct.[13] Crucially, it is the first scholarly publication that elaborates the basic geographical distinctions of continents that Linneaus and others will later assert as the lands of different races of man.

This book first piqued my interest because it was an example of a book that represented the colonial ventures to not only the Americas, but also India and Africa all in one text. It demonstrated a simple, yet important and often overlooked aspect of colonial discourse: whereas most people writing about this time often consider "Indians" in relation to "Europeans," or "Africans" in relation to "Europeans," or to put it in terms more common today Indian/White, Black/White relations, narratives regarding "Indians" were mediated through not only a contrast to an emerging concept of "the European," but also in close relation to discourses of blackness and orientalism.

Paesi Nouamente Retrovati was the first book of its kind to find a wide audience and be immediately translated from Italian into Latin, German, and French in subsequent years,[14] reflecting its popularity at the time. Although extremely popular during the height of its circulation, the book has been largely forgotten outside of small academic circles. *Paesi Nouamente Retrovati* is, however, widely regarded as the founding example that other collections of colonial narratives would follow, from Peter de Martyr's *De Orbe Novo* (*On the New World*) to Battista Ramusio's *Delle Navigazioni et Viaggi* (*Navigations and Travel).*[15] Much has been written about these later books, in which many of the letters examined here were included, but none focus on the gendered and sexualized content. Beyond a few brief references,

I have found nothing in English analyzing *Paesi* as a whole. This chapter is the first in-depth study written of *Paesi Nouamente Retrovati* (1507), in which I examine the deployment of sexuality and gender in the production of geopolitical difference; that is, how discourses of sexuality and gender were key in concretizing the emerging distinctions between Africans, Amerindians, East Indians, and Europeans. I then elaborate how the legacy of *Paesi*, through Ramusio's *Navigazioni*, shaped Richard Hakluyt's English nationalist *The Principal Navigations*.

Specifically, *Paesi Nouamente Retrovati* includes selected letters from the voyages to the following regions: Alvise Cadamosto and Pedro de Sintra to western Africa, the travels of Pedro Alvarez Cabral to western Africa, Brazil, and India, and letters from Christopher Columbus and Amerigo Vespucci's respective voyages to the Americas.

ACTS OF DIFFERENTIATION

The very naming of the people of the Americas as "Indian," and the continued use of this term even after the realization that this land was not in fact anywhere in the world previously known to Europeans, signals the level upon which the people of the Americas were being integrated into European discourse. There are many aspects to this history, and this is but one, however it is an important one not to overlook for it foregrounds the relational context in which continental ontologies gained their coherency.

The term "Indian" was used interchangeably with the names "Kush" and "Ethiopia" since antiquity to the modern period in Greco-Roman, Jewish, Christian, and Islamic texts.[16] For example, Herodutus who wrote in the fifth century BC called Indians "Ethiopians," distinguishing only between "wooly-haired Ethiopians" and "straight-haired Ethiopians." The terms Ethiopian and Indian were also used interchangeably in the travel writings of Marco Polo, written in 1298. Petrus Alliacus' *Imago Mundi* from 1410, the book that Christopher Columbus carried with him on his voyages across the Atlantic, similarly refers to "two Ethiopias."[17] It is this historical context of the interchangeable usage of the words "Indian" and "Ethiopian" that, I think, offers some insight into the ensuing naming and treatment of the people of the Americas.

Although not all slaves in Europe were black at the time of contact, the African slave trade was expanding, and there was a growing correlation being made that all Africans, that is "Ethiopians," were meant to be slaves.[18] The interchangeability of terms used to denote a wide variety of peoples points to the ambiguous nature of defining unfamiliar people, and not in discrete continental categories, at this time.

SEXUALITY, GENDER, AND EARLY ENCOUNTERS: AFRICA (1456)

Anne McClintock's book, *Imperial Leather* makes the insightful observation that "[A]s European men crossed the dangerous thresholds of their known worlds, they ritualistically feminized borders and boundaries. Female figures were planted like fetishes at the ambiguous points of contact, at the borders and orifices of the contest zone."[19] McClintock's words find strong resonance in *Paesi Nouamente Retrovati*. In the opening letter of Alvise Cadamosto, he speaks of a young woman of the Kingdom of Senega (what is now called Senegal). The exchange is between Cadamosto and the King of Senega, and the object of exchange is a young woman. His letter reads:

> He besought me to go inland to his house, about two hundred and fifty miles from the shore.[20] There he would reward me richly, and I might remain for some days, for he had promised me one hundred slaves in return for what he had received. I gave him the horses with their harness and other goods, which together had cost me originally about three hundred ducats. I therefore decided to go with him, but before I left he gave me a handsome young *negro* girl, twelve years of age, saying that he gave her to me for the service of my chamber. I accepted her and sent her to my ship. My journey inland was indeed more to see interesting sights and obtain information, than to receive my dues.[21]

The reference to the young woman to be "in the service of" Cadamosto's chamber situates her nameless body as the boundary port-of-entry, through which Cadamosto will see interesting sights and obtain information. Her agency and subjectivity are displaced as a representation of the passive land upon which he will "journey inland." The affectation in mentioning the girl's young age suggests her virginity, invoking the land as female *and* virginal, awaiting the arrival of a (European) man. Through the enunciation of this passage, Cadamosto verbally positions himself as an agent of power in relation to the Kingdom of Senega all while the young, virginal, black woman serves as the border entryway that will be transgressed for his pleasure and enrichment.

Sexuality and subjugation are deeply entwined in the face-to-face relations narrated by Cadamosto. In the first pages of his narrative, he speaks of how he has gained information about the sexuality of Canarians from slave raiders who have captured men and women from the islands.[22] A few pages later, Cadamosto's fantasy of sexual promiscuity and incest among West Africans works in tandem with his descriptions of idolatry, heathenism, skin color, and inferior intelligence and character. These representations serve to construct the emerging black subject in contrast to what is presented deceptively as a presumably natural European norm. The European norm is in contrast defined as Christian, patriarchal, monogamous, masculinist, and of superior human stock. Cadamosto narrates:

> In this place Budomel had nine wives: and likewise in his other dwellings, according to his will and pleasure. Each of these wives has five or six young black girls in attendance upon her, and it is as lawful for the lord to sleep with these attendants as with his wives, to whom this does not appear an injury, for it is customary. In this way the lord changes frequently. These *negros*, both men and women, are exceedingly lascivious: Budomel demanded of me importunately, having been given to understand that Christians knew how to do many things, whether by chance I could give him the means by which he could satisfy many women, for which he offered me a great reward. They are also very jealous, and allow no one to enter the huts where their wives live—not even trusting their own sons.[23]

In Cadamosto's narrative, one of the central characteristics that define western Africans as not-Portuguese is their sexual practices, which include the possibility of sexual intimacy between mother and son. We can see here the establishment of a myth of perversity in western African social life by suggesting they are incestuous, implicitly establishing chastity as a European norm.

CANNIBALISM AND THE "NEW WORLD" TEXTUAL ECONOMY

Turning away from the initial letters of Cadamosto, the letters included in *Paesi* cover a variety of areas, yet the themes of gender and sexuality are persistent.

Another one of the more persistent early images of people of the Americas is that of "the cannibal," that is the commercial representation of people who take pleasure in the consumption of another human's flesh. Throughout the letters written by Columbus himself, as well as a letter written by a Dr. Diego Alvarez Chanca who accompanied Columbus across the Atlantic, incidents are recounted as evidence of the man-eating habits of Amerindians.[24] Whether these narratives are true or not has been the focus of years of debate with no sight of conclusive evidence forthcoming,[25] however, their efficacy in demarcating Indian people as a sub-human group in the early days of colonization cannot be denied. My focus, therefore, is not on whether there was cannibalism or not, but rather on analyzing the effects of the centrality and persistence of cannibalism in representations of the Americas from the first accounts of the "New World."

First, to understand the implications of Columbus and Alvarez Chanca's letters it is useful to relate the earliest reports of man-eating peoples that the two men were familiar with. The earliest written account of a man-eating people is from Pomponius Mela in 50 AD. Mela writes:

> In the *furthest* east of Asia are the Indians, Seres, and Scythians. The Indians and Scythians occupy the two *extremities*, the Seres are in the middle. . . . That part which adjoins the Scythian promontory is impassable from snow; then follows an uncultivated tract occupied by savages. These tribes are the man-eating Scythians and the Sakas, severed from one another by a region where none can dwell because of the number of wild animals.[26]

Similar to depictions of Africa as the "ends of the earth," the Scythians live on the outmost regions of the "east" in an equally *remote* area in the lands we now call Iran. Pliny, a friend of Mela and also an historian writing around 50 AD with whom Christopher Columbus was familiar,[27] describes the Scythians in the following passage:

> The first portion of these shores, after we pass the Scythian Promontory, is totally uninhabitable, owing to the snow, and the regions adjoining are uncultivated, in consequence of the savage state of the nations that dwell there. Here are the abodes of the Scythian man-eaters who feed on human flesh. Hence it is that all around them consists of vast deserts, inhabited by multitudes of wild beasts, which are continually lying in wait, ready to fall upon human beings just as savage as themselves.[28]

These earliest accounts of a savage, beastlike, man-eating people in the farthest eastern reaches of the known world are what identify and distinguish "humans" from inhuman others.[29] It is this abstract conceptual relationship between human/sub-human that creates the conditions for articulating a coherent Western European Christian identity. What I want to draw your attention to in this instance, is that when contrasted with the future letters about the Americas, the accounts from Pomponius Mela and Pliny are noticeably non-gender specific.

The representations of Indians in the "New World" as cannibals *in an explicitly gendered rendering* establish a unique boundary between savage and civilized. Crucially, not only is a gendered demarcation introduced, but the sex/gender anatomical matrix ascribed to "true patriarchies" is inverted. Bodies assigned a male sex are gendered female, and bodies assigned a female sex are gendered male. It is because of this history that we cannot assume that what appears as sexual dimorphism or is presumed to be heterosexuality in the colonial context holds the same symbolic codes across the modern/colonial gender system, nor that the patriarchal distribution of power is smooth across the colonial/racial divide.[30] These points have been raised by women of color feminists many times in the contemporary context, but this research on early representation brings out the historical scope of the situation.[31] It highlights that the struggles over sexual and gendered autonomy among the damnés is not a struggle limited to the post-Enlightenment period. The interpretation of classical texts in sixteenth-century colonial knowledge production introduced a new semiotics of sex and gender that persists to this day: a Manichean division across the colonial divide.

The sharp divisions constructed between "man" and "woman" throughout the Christian Bible and later secularly reinforced and modified by the recovered texts of Aristotle are newly mobilized in *Paesi*'s novel rendering of man-eating peoples.[32] Note this quote from Dr. Chanca's letter to the queen about Columbus's second voyage, describing what he claims the Carib Indians do to other people on the islands:

> These women also say that they are treated with a cruelty, which appears to be incredible, for they eat the male children whom they have from them and only rear those whom they have from their own women. As for the men whom they are able to take, they bring such as are alive to their houses to cut up for meat, and those who are dead, they eat at once. They say that the flesh

Figure 3.1 Sixteenth-century artist, Hans Staden. 1557. Woodcut, original at the John Carter Brown Library at Brown University.

> of a man is so good that there is nothing like it in the world, and it certainly seems to be so for, from the bones which we found in their houses, they had gnawed everything that could be gnawed, so that nothing was left on them except what was too tough to be eaten. In one house there a neck of a man was found cooking in a pot. They castrate the boys whom they capture and employ them as servants until they are full grown, and then when they wish to make a feast, they kill and eat them, for they say that the flesh of boys and of women is not good to eat. Of these boys, three came fleeing to us, and all three had been castrated.[33]

An image of a life lived in extraordinary perversity is created in this account.

Chanca's letter marks an important moment in colonial discourse and a departure from earlier Greek narratives: the explicit imagery of gendered violence emerges as a way in which to elaborate the state of degeneration of the people encountered. In this fabulation of Amerindian society men are the "weaker sex" and the chaos caused by this inversion of so-called natural law is on display for all to see.

Figure 3.2 Sixteenth-century artist, America, Part 3. 1593. Woodcut, original at the John Carter Brown Library at Brown University.

Now this image that you can see in Figure 3.3 was created by Theodor De Bry and printed in 1593, more than one hundred years after the printing of Chanca's letter. It was actually inspired by a 1578 book, *History of a Voyage to the Land of Brazil,* written by Jean de Lery, a French Protestant man, similar in many ways to the 1557 book, *True History and Description of a Land Belonging to the Wild, Naked, Savage, Man-munching People, Situated in the New World, America,* written by a German man named Hans Staden upon his return from Brazil (Figure 3.1). What I want to emphasize here is that what may have started as an individual, hand written, letter to the Spanish Crown by Dr. Chanca, was printed and reprinted, along with other narratives, and then large, lavishly illustrated series by artists such as De Bry were also produced. Together, the narratives and images, in effect, produced a regime of representation that would form the backdrop for the debates about whether peoples in the Americas were human at all.

These discovery narratives were being reproduced by elite European men at the same time as the human status of the people of Africa and the Americas was being debated. This was the debate between theologians Juan Gines

Figure 3.3 Sixteenth-century artist, America, Part 3. 1593. Woodcut, original at the John Carter Brown Library at Brown University.

de Sepulveda and Bartolomé de las Casas, known as the Valladolid debate, that concluded that Africans were natural slaves, that Indians were natural children, and Europeans the only fully human beings.[34] The misanthropic hierarchical classification of the human was taken as a framework for the organization of the *sistema de castas* and apportioning value to people's lives based on this hierarchy. The conclusion of the Valladolid debate is also the basis of Sylvia Wynter's thesis on the triadic schema.

SEXUALITY, GENDER, AND THE COLONIAL ENCOUNTER

> Colonialism did not impose pre-colonial, European gender arrangements on the colonized. It imposed a new gender system. . . . It introduced many genders and gender itself as a colonial concept and mode of organization of relations of production, property relations, cosmologies and ways of knowing.[35]
>
> —María Lugones

Columbus himself wrote another letter that appears in *Paesi*, and it became one of the most famous records from the early colonial period. In it, Columbus describes the people of the Americas both in contrast to, and in relation with Africans and uses highly sexualized and gendered language. He compares Indian people to the people of Guinea in West Africa distinguished only by their straight hair. Columbus also describes the people he encounters as cowardly, innocent, keenly intelligent, cannibalistic, and sexually deviant. Columbus writes:

> They are no more malformed than the others, except that they have the custom of wearing their hair long like women, and they use bows and arrows of cane stems. . . . These are those who have intercourse with the women of Matinino,[36] which is the first island met on the way from Spain to the Indies, in which there is not a man. These women engage in no feminine occupation, but use bows and arrows of cane like those already mentioned, and arm and protect themselves with plates of copper, of which they have much.[37]

This allusion to an island inhabited by Amazon women is important. The Amazons of Greek myth, believed to live in Africa and Asia, are described in those myths as "a people who excelled at war . . . and if they ever had intercourse with men and gave birth to children, they only raised the girls."[38] They were also known for going to war and killing many Greeks. Amazons are further described as living in ends-of-the-earth locations. Such a description implicitly connotes an external and subordinate position in the Greco imaginary, for it was believed that the farther one was from the Mediterranean "heartland" the more degenerate one's culture was.[39] In Greek society only men went to war, and so "Amazons symbolize what in the *polis* is a normative masculinity."[40]

Their placement at the edge of the known world "is a spatial expression of their reversal of patriarchal culture: Amazons blur the categories that classify the domains of male and female."[41] They further represent a "structural reversal of the paradigm of civilization and the organization of power."[42] In other words, at the edges of the known world, in this case what was believed to be the peripheral islands off the coast of mainland China, the binaries of human/divine, human/animal, or male/female are being interpreted in unique form. It is here that Columbus is locating what would become known as the Caribbean.

The particular organization of gender in Columbus' letter provides a concrete example of the different history that a decolonial feminism would need to account for in contrast to the legacy of the middle-class white feminist movement. Rather than women being characterized as "fragile, weak in both body and mind, secluded in the private, and sexually passive" as white bourgeois women were, "Amazons of the Caribbean" were out in public, strong in body, aggressive, and sexually assertive (see Figure 3.4). Based on these letters, the men of the Amazons could not claim authority and did not

Figure 3.4 Anonymous sixteenth-century artist, Amazons Killing Men (Guianas), 1599. Woodcut, original at the John Carter Brown Library at Brown University.

have control over production or reproduction, two key attributes of bourgeois white masculinity.[43] A close examination of the discovery letters in *Paesi*, uniquely organized in an edited volume, demonstrates the historical specificity of gender systems across the colonial divide.

The imagined hypersexuality of women in the Americas was not attributed to the isolated behavior of a few individual miscreants, but rather, was written as constitutive of who they were as a people. Furthermore, the sexual romps and consumption of human flesh in the images about the Americas was not perceived by church authorities as an excess of Christian *male* sexuality, as was the case with European erotica,[44] but rather as truth-building depictions of a society in which women were primary sexual instigators.

Early colonial print culture's imaginary regarding women in the Americas as those who perform the sexual roles *normally* attributed to European Christian men, at once attributed normative masculine characteristics to those deemed morphologically women and normative feminine characteristics to those deemed morphologically men, thus casting them as phenotypically Indian. The Indian phenotype, so to speak, was a sex/gender role-inverted people specific to a geographic location. Simultaneously, the narratives implicitly demarcate heteronormativity as the purview of those in God's company: that is Christian Europeans.

Another important aspect of these tales of Amazons and sexually licentious men and women in the Americas were not only interpreted as the markers of a distinct human type, but also conversely, as narratives of a freer society. Peter Linebaugh and Marcus Redicker state in *The Many-Headed Hydra: The Hidden History of the Revolutionary Atlantic* that these reports about the Americas, "inflamed the collective imagination of Europe, inspiring endless discussion—among statesmen, philosophers, and writers, as well as the dispossessed."[45] In addition to the idea that in the Americas lived a people without property, work, masters, or kings, also lived the idea that a people were more sexually liberated there. For some, these discovery narratives invoked dreams of utopia. The double move between dehumanization and exaltation is definitive of the work of stereotyping. Behind racial hatred is desire. The fear of the desire for the constructed subhuman is rendered in the mechanically produced image of the Indian woman who has the potential to literally consume the European male body: penis, limbs, torso, and head.

THE REPRODUCTION OF THE "NEW WORLD"

These texts and images, originally written and drawn by individuals, were then transferred into typeface and woodcut blocks, printed, and circulated widely. The printing press facilitated the process of integrating these texts and images into a system of representation. In fact, this was one of *the* key impacts the printing press had on the production and circulation of knowledge in western and northern Europe. Images, maps, and diagrams could be mechanically reproduced in quantities larger than previously seen, and at a speed faster than ever possible, creating the opportunity of an "exactly repeatable pictorial statement."[46]

In the groundbreaking book, *The Printing Press as an Agent of Change*, Elizabeth Eisenstein argues that typography arrested linguistic drift, meaning that the print machine helped enrich as well as standardize vernaculars, and paved the way for the more deliberate purification and codification of all major European languages. Eisenstein discusses these themes as they relate to shifts in labor dynamics and religious and scientific revolutions. Knowledge production was organized around this new medium.

The new terms in which knowledge production was organized, specifically the centralization of printing presses in cities in Europe and the regulation of what could be said and by whom, created the conditions for the unequal circulation of perspectives and insights from across the colonial divide. It was against the backdrop of standardization, purification, codification, and nationalization in European book production that, for example, Hernan Cortez was ordering the *destruction* of Nahuatl books and records. In fact, in 1573 the Spanish Crown went so far as to illegalize any written reference to indigenous ways of knowing. An edict was issued stating, "Under no consideration should any person whatsoever write things touching on the superstitions and manner of life which these Indians formerly had."[47] So the unrestrained proliferation of books such as *Paesi Nouamente Retrovati* that distributed stereotypical narratives of Amazons and cannibals in the Americas, was paralleled by the prohibition of reproducing books detailing indigenous thought, particularly those written by indigenous peoples themselves.

The effect of an "exactly repeatable pictorial statement" that for the most part only represented the Americas in highly problematic ways was that it standardized and reproduced words and images about people in the Americas, manipulating the lens through which a subject could be understood, even delimiting what aspects could be thought about. This phenomenon, coupled with the dissemination of the printed book to a scattered array of readers, helps explain the conditions for producing early stereotypes.

As new editions and translations of books regarding the Americas were printed, there remained a steadfast representation of the people as (for example) lawless cannibals and societies of Amazons. These reproductions were a key aspect of the material conditions for producing a stereotypical notion of people in the Americas.

To put this in a global context: just as printing favored the growth of the Reformation, so it helped mold modern European languages. During the sixteenth century, there took place a process of unification and consolidation that established fairly large territories wherein a single language was written.[48] The contemporary development of the idea of a "territorial language" which would later transform into the "national language," as they exist today, was happening at the same time and in response to the encounters with southern Africa, the Americas, and India. While modern European languages were defining themselves into heterogeneous, autonomous entities there was also the simultaneous process of defining the people of the Americas as homogenous, abnormally gendered, and subordinate to Europeans generally. Arguably, the dissolution of a common Latin culture was replaced by the affirmations of local difference in Rome, Italy, Germany, France, Spain, and Britain, all consolidated in part by the printing press.[49] Yet this shift did not signal the total collapse of a sense of a shared location in the world. What we see, instead, is the rise of an implicitly gendered notion of "the European" taking firm hold.

The monies that were flowing into the countries of Spain and France from the new colonies were facilitating the centralization of "national" monarchies, and publishers wanting to ever expand their markets encouraged the standardization of languages over a large area so as to be able to sell their products as easily and cheaply to as wide an audience as possible.[50] All this was occurring in the context of trans-Atlantic expansion, a growing African slave trade, Indian hyperexploitation and the establishment of new colonies where literacy was regulated to only perpetuate European systems of power.[51]

The gendered discourse in books regarding Indigenous peoples of the Americas would have a lasting negative impact and would be key to the solidification of a particular notion of European masculinity. What we commonly refer to today as differences of race, gender, sexuality, and economy must be recognized not as entirely separate categories that intersect only occasionally, but rather as always already intertwined categorizations across difference with a shared history in the colonization of the Americas and the expansion of the Atlantic slave trade.

RAMUSIO'S *DELLE NAVIGAZIONI ET VIAGGI*

The impact of Montalboddo's *Paesi Nouamente Retrovati* is evident in Giovanni Battista Ramusio's collection of books titled *Navigazioni e Viaggi* published in three separate volumes in 1550, 1559, and 1606. The collection was inspired by *Paesi* and Ramusio followed a similar objective, but his collection is significantly larger, spanning hundreds of pages. The same themes regarding Africa, India, and the Americas are included in *Navigazioni*, but Ramusio added accounts of the Persian Empire and Eastern Europe in his assemblage of texts. At the time that Ramusio was editing the accounts, Italy was in the middle of a war between the monarchies of Western Europe vying for control of Italy.[52] For this reason, at one point Ramusio refers to Italy as a miserable nation.[53] Ramusio's stated purpose was to provide accounts that would help create a more accurate world map on regions not adequately covered in Ptolemy's classical text *Geography*.

One set of letters that Ramusio includes is of Josafa Barbaro, a Renaissance Italian ambassador and merchant. In these letters of the Persian Empire and Eastern Europe, Circassians are derided as not being men, but like women, and thus conquerable. A story dated 1486 is told of Muslims slaughtering Christians, including women and children, underscoring the "miserable state" Christians endure in these parts. Another vivid account, dated 1487, is of Muslims attempting—and failing—to convert a Christian, testifying to the virtue of the Christians in this area. Barbaro concludes Muslims are a "barbarous people, ignorant of all good manners and full of evil customs."[54] It is unclear how Barbaro differentiates between "good" and "evil" Persians, although the differentiation is consistently made. It is possible he is differentiating between Christian Persians from other religious groups, but who exactly is not specified and so cannot be presumed. He sometimes refers to them as "well behaved and of gentle manners, and by their conduct appear to be like Christians."[55] This is the same description that Caterino Zeno, another Venetian diplomat, offers in another letter included in *Navigazioni*.[56] There are a few occasions that narratives of sexuality are mentioned. Two of the stories are of the same man, an emperor named Ussuncassan whose second wife has a son that meets an unfortunate end. The letter of Ambrosio Contarini says the son conspired against his father and thus has to be put to death by him.[57] The second letter, by Giovanni Maria Angiolello, says the son was killed after the father's death by the three sons of his first wife.[58] Another story is of a nameless woman of "lascivious disposition," described only as the daughter of the Lord of San Mutra. She lusts to marry another man, and so tries to kill her current husband. Her plan is foiled, however, and she ends up not only killing her husband, but her son and herself.[59] The fourth story of multiple wives also has a tragic end for a son. Ismail, a direct descendent of Mohammed the Prophet, is very popular and loved by the people. Concerned that he holds too much sway, the father imprisons him, and he spends most of his life there so that he cannot usurp the Sultans' power.[60] Based on these stories there appears to be a dire warning: polygamy will spell disaster for a son.

A fascinating section in Ramusio's texts is when he is pondering the meaning of all the accounts and what this novel moment in the history of the world means. He states,

> Everyone who considers the various changes brought by the course of events to human affairs, will, on reflection, be filled with wonder; but I think that those who read ancient history have greater reason to be so, seeing many republics and many great and powerful kingdoms, so to speak, collapse without, in certain cases, leaving even a name, or any memorial behind. The same course of events has caused many races to leave their native countries, and, like proud and rapid rivers, invade those of others, chasing away the ancient inhabitants, and, not content with that, even change their names. So it happens that, nowadays, there are many races whose origin is not known, of which miserable Italy is an example.[61]

Ramusio acknowledges that his collection is a narration of colonialism, and he is aware that it is a violent process involving the removal of people from their land and then renaming those lands in the name of the colonizers. Natal alienation is characteristic as removed peoples are left with no known origin. Yet Ramusio's response is in bad faith. He immediately attributes the patterns of colonization to nature, likening it to the power of a rapid river. This is a clear indication of Ramusio's abnegation of his and other people's agency in the process of colonization. Ramusio also names England as a colonized territory. The move here is a crucial one, as it is a logic that justifies colonialism and will be used by generations to come to excuse the acts of contemporary colonizations. By rendering modern colonialism to an ahistorical cycle beyond human agency, Ramusio rescinds the conscious decisions made to enact or refuse colonialism. Colonialism is, fundamentally, a particular way of enacting relationships with people that subjugates and/or murders some while glorifying and indulging others, however, it is too soon for Ramusio to foresee that racialized capitalism will characterize modern colonialism. There is a precedent that is clearly established at this early time by these texts, and that is situating western European men as the agent, the observer, and the first point of reference regarding culture and knowledge in Western knowledge production. This is a pattern that will be replicated throughout modern academia until the decolonial revolts of the mid-twentieth century.[62]

HAKLUYT'S *PRINCIPAL NAVIGATIONS*

It was Ramusio's *Della Navigationi et Viaggi* that English nationalist Richard Hakluyt would use as his reference guide to create *The Principal Navigations* of 1589. He replicated many of the accounts of Ramusio who had replicated them from Montalboddo, as well as providing new and different accounts. *The Principal Navigations* would be a sixteen-volume collection with an explicit agenda: to spur the English colonial project.[63] What is of note for this study is how the same accounts of gender and sexuality that were produced very early in the century continued to circulate and find new life not only across generations but across colonial projects and languages. It is a clear example of how the English colonial project was influenced by the Spanish. Although Hakluyt's agenda was to compete and usurp the Spanish, he held onto the perspectives and assumptions that the Spanish made regarding the people encountered. The main change Hakluyt made was to supplant the centrality of Spanish colonialism with English aspirations, but the narratives are structurally very similarly. For example, Thomas Cavendish's narrative (an English explorer) writes about the Philippines sometime between 1586 and 1588:

> Every man and man-child among them hath a nail of tin thrust quite through the head of his privy part, being split in the lower end and rivetted, and on the head of the nail is as it were a crown: which is driven through their privities when they be young, and the place groweth up again, without any great pain to the child: and they take this nail out and in, as occasion serveth. . . . This custom was granted at the request of the women of the country, who finding their men to be given to the foul sin of sodomy, desired some remedy against that mischief. . . . These people wholly worship the devil, and often times have conference with him, which appeareth unto them in ugly and monstrous shape.[64]

It is difficult to detect any significant difference between the substance of the Spanish colonial narratives and of the British in their discussions of racialized sexuality. Hakluyt's work went on to inspire the next generation of travel writers, Theodor de Bry and Jean de Thévenot. And yet, in all these books of travels very little is said of the so-called mixed race people who are being produced at the same time. Hakluyt does include the mention of one mestizo in Java, who is described as half Indian and half Portuguese, but given that descriptions of the people and the lands traveled are the focus of these books, why not describe the "mixed" peoples too?[65]

The logic of continental ontologies emerged and circulated between Spanish and English colonists through these texts, but the "mixed race" people being produced were invisibilized in the intellectual elaborations of racial/continental differences. This has created a disjuncture between colonial scholarly production and the reality of colonial struggles over land and labor in the Americas. The implications of this are still felt today as we turn to colonial documents as a main source of history and theory, but then struggle to sufficiently understand and explain the sociogeny of natally alienated *castas*.

By way of conclusion, the link between the representations of "Indian," "African," "Asian," and "European" people as mutually constitutive, which I have sought to elucidate herein, is an important constitutive feature for the examination of the coloniality of being. The sexual dynamic, specifically the overrepresentation of people as Amazons, cannibals, and lascivious women as so clearly illustrated in early woodcuts and books, such as *Paesi Nouamente Retrovati* (1507), *Delle Navigazioni et Viaggi* (1550, 1559, 1606), and *The Principal Navigations* (1589), were constitutive in the emergence of ideas surrounding the Americas, and in the emergence of notions of continental ontologies as a dominant organizing principle of social and economic relations. Examining the key role of sexuality and gender in the early representation of "the Americas" exposes them as playing a key role in justifying and even naturalizing trans-Atlantic violence. In so doing, it brings forth the possibility of asking new or more nuanced questions with regards to gender and sexuality across the colonial/racial divide.

Furthermore, we can see that these early colonial key texts never addressed the growing "mixed" population who were being regulated and codified as distinct from their "continental groups." This practice of excluding *castas* in studies of colonized ontology would be continued on through the eighteenth and nineteenth centuries of scientific racism. And now, critical and decolonial engagements with these narratives often replicate the same categories without reconsidering the lived reality. In a contemporary context, working class *castas* who identify their histories as natally alienated colonial/racial subjects have to do the critical work of connecting individual experiences to a systematic structural analysis, and developing a decolonial praxis to underscore the process of becoming that is being human.

NOTES

1. Simone de Beauvoir, *The Second Sex* (New York: Vintage Books, 1989), xxi.
2. Simone de Beauvoir, *The Second Sex* (New York: Vintage Books, 1989), 720–21.
3. David Hulchanski, *The Three Cities Within Toronto: Income Polarization Among Toronto's Neighborhoods, 1970–2005* (Toronto: Cities Centre Press, University of Toronto, 2010); Ruthie Gilmore, *The Golden Gulag: Prisons, Surplus, Crisis, and Opposition in Globalizing California* (Berkeley: University of California Press, 2007).
4. See Orlando Patterson, *Slavery and Social Death: A Comparative Study* (Cambridge, MA: Harvard University Press, 1982).
5. See Robert Sokolowski, *Husserlian Meditations: How Words Present Things* (Evanston, IL: Northwestern University Press, 1974).
6. Theories by Homer, Aristotle, Mallos, and Ptolemy were debated. See W. G. L. Randles, "Classical Models of World Geography and Their Transformation Following the Discovery of America," in *The Classical Tradition and the Americas*, ed. Wolfgang Haase and Meyer Reinhold (New York: Walter de Gruyter & Co., 1993). See also Martin W. Lewis and Karen Wigen, *The Myth of Continents: A Critique of Metageography* (Berkeley: University of California Press, 1997).

7. See Marshall Hodgson, *The Venture of Islam Vol. 1, 2 and 3* (Chicago: The University of Chicago Press, 1977); Janet Abu Lughod, *Before European Hegemony: The World System A.D. 1250–1350* (New York: Oxford University Press, 1989); Colin Imber, *The Ottoman Empire, 1300–1650: The Structure of Power* (New York: Palgrave Macmillan, 2002).

8. Karl Marx and Friedrich Engels, *The Communist Manifesto* (New York: International Publishers Co., 2014), 1.

9. Lucien Febvre and Henri-Jean Martin, *The Coming of the Book: The Impact of Printing 1450–1800* (New York: Verso, 1997).

10. In G. R. Crone, ed., *The Voyages of Cadamosto and Other Documents on Western Africa in the Second Half of the Fifteenth Century* (London: Hakluyt Society, 1937), 20.

11. Ibid., 208.

12. Fracanzano da Montalboddo, *Paesi Nouamente Retrovati & Novo Mondo da Alberico Vesputio Florentino Intitulato* (Princeton, NJ: Princeton University Press, 1916). *Paesi Nouamente Retrovati* (1507) was published a full seventy-five years prior to the publication of Richard Hakluyt's, *Divers Voyages Touching the Discoverie of America* (1582) and ninety-one years before *The Principall Navigations, Voiages, and Discoveries of the English Nation* (1598). *Paesi Nouamente Retrovati* also found wide circulation eighty years prior to Theodor de Bry's *Les Grands Voyages, India Orientalische and India Occidentalische* (1588).

13. Edward Said, *Orientalism* (New York: Vintage Books, 1979), 12.

14. Crone, *The Voyage of Cadamosto*, xliii.

15. Francis Augustus MacNutt, *De Orbe Novo: The Right Decades of Peter Martyr D' Anghera* (New York: G. P. Putnam's Sons, 1912); Giovanni Battista Ramusio, *Delle Navigazioni e Viaggi* (*Navigations and Travel)* (Torino: G. Einaudi, 1978).

16. David M. Goldenberg, *The Curse of Ham: Race and Slavery in Early Judaism, Christianity, and Islam* (Princeton, NJ: Princeton University Press, 2003), 212.

17. Petrus de Alliacus, *Imago Mundi* (Boston: Massachussetts Historical Society, 1927), ch. 37.

18. This story from the Bible has been the main justification for the African slave trade and would be used as late as 1838 to argue the inherent subordinate status of black Africans. See Goldenberg, *The Curse of Ham*, 1.

19. Anne McClintock, *Imperial Leather: Race, Gender and Sexuality in the Colonial Conquest* (New York: Routledge, 1995), 24.

20. The community was actually twenty-five miles inwards, not 250 miles.

21. Crone, *The Voyages of Cadamosto*, 36.

22. Ibid., 13.

23. Ibid., 38.

24. Chanca, "The Second Voyage of Columbus," 26–32.

25. See for example, William Arens, *The Man-Eating Myth: Anthropology and Anthropophagy* (New York: Oxford University Press, 1979); Frank Lestringant, *Cannibals: The Discovery and Representation of the Cannibal from Columbus to Jules Verne* (Berkeley: University of California Press, 1997); Patricia Seed, *American Pentimento: The Invention of Indians and the Pursuit of Riches* (Minneapolis: University of Minnesota Press, 2001).

26. Pomponius Mela, *De situ orbis, libri tres* (Salamanca: Diego Cussío, 1598), 7.

27. Columbus was known to have taken a copy of Petrus Alliacus' *Imago Mundi*, originally written in 1410, with him on his voyages. *Imago Mundi* is a book that draws from Pliny to a great extent. It was this book by Alliacus that gave encouragement to Columbus to travel new routes across the Atlantic. For further detail see George Nunn, "The Imago Mundi and Columbus," *The American Historical Review* 40, no. 4 (July 1935): 646–61.

28. Pliny the Elder, *Pliny's Natural History: A Selection from Philemon Holland's Translation* (Oxford: Clarendon Press, 1964), 36.

29. Susan M. Kim, "Man-Eating Monsters and Ants as Big as Dogs," in *Animals and the Symbolic in Mediaeval Art and Literature* (Groningen: Egbert Forsten, 1997), 39.

30. Maria Lugones, "The Coloniality of Gender," *Worlds & Knowledges Otherwise* 2 (April 2008): 5. The collusion of colonial/racial subjects sexed and/or gendered as male with white patriarchy is a betrayal.

31. Cathy J. Cohen, "Punks, Bulldaggers, and Welfare Queens," *GLQ: A Journal of Lesbian and Gay Studies* 3 (May 1997): 437–65.

32. See Aristotle, *Generation of Animals*, 716a5–23, 727a2–30, 727b31–33, 728b18–31, 765b8–20, 766a17–30, 783b29–784a12. For further discussion on European scholars' reintroduction to Aristotle's works, see Norman Kretzmann, Anthony Kenny, and Jan Pinborg, eds., *The Cambridge History of Later Medieval Philosophy: From the Rediscovery of Aristotle to the Disintegration of Scholasticism, 1100–1600* (Cambridge: Cambridge University Press, 1988), 45–98.

33. Diego Alvarez Chanca, "Second Voyage of Columbus," in *Select Documents Illustrating the Four Voyages of Columbus: Volume 1* (London: Hakluyt Society, 1930), 32.

34. See Anthony Pagden, *The Fall of Natural Man: The American Indian and the Origins of Comparative Ethnology* (Cambridge: Cambridge University Press, 1982), 57–108.

35. Lugones, "Heterosexualism and the Colonial/Modern Gender System," 186.

36. Later renamed Martinique.

37. Christopher Columbus, "First Voyage of Columbus," in *Select Documents Illustrating the Four Voyages of Columbus: Volume 1* (London: Hakluyt Society, 1930), 16.

38. Apollodorus, *The Library of Greek Mythology* (New York: Oxford University Press, 1997), 78.

39. Margaret T. Hodgen, *Early Anthropology in the Sixteenth and Seventeenth Centuries* (Philadelphia: University of Pennsylvania Press, 1964), 255.

40. V. Y. Mudimbe, *The Idea of Africa: Gnosis, Philosophy, and the Order of Knowledge* (Bloomington: Indiana University Press, 1994), 84.

41. William Blake Tyrrell, *Amazons: A Study in Athenian Mythmaking* (Baltimore: Johns Hopkins University Press, 1984), 57.

42. Mudimbe, *The Idea of Africa*, 80–92.

43. Lugones, "Heterosexualism and the Modern World System," 202.

44. Karras explains that male sexuality was understood to always want to go beyond the boundaries of proper behavior and therefore sometimes in need of being reeled in. Karras, *Sexuality in Medieval Europe*, 120–49.

45. Peter Linebaugh and Marcus Redicker, *The Many-Headed Hydra: The Hidden History of the Revolutionary Atlantic* (Boston: Beacon Press, 2001), 24. See also, Stephen Greenblatt, *Renaissance Self-Fashioning: From More to Shakespeare* (Chicago: The University of Chicago Press, 2005).

46. See William M. Ivins Jr., *Prints and Visual Communication* (Cambridge, MA: Harvard University Press, 1953).

47. Lewis Hanke, *Bartolomé de Las Casas: Bookman, Scholar and Propagandist* (Philadelphia: University of Philadelphia Press, 1952), 29.

48. Febvre and Martin, *The Coming of the Book*, 319.

49. Febvre and Martin end their book lamenting about the fragmentation of the world of letters by the 1600s. They ask: "What did the French know about Shakespeare in the 17th century? Or about contemporary German writing in the 18th century?" This may be true but it does not mean the provincializing of their privilege and power in the production of knowledge on a global scale, quite the opposite—they soon become the centers of power, equally implicated in the global production of knowledge about "Europe" vis-à-vis non-Europe. See Febvre and Martin, *The Coming of the Book*, 332.

50. Ibid., 320.

51. See Robert T. Jiménez, *The History of Reading and the Uses of Literacy in Colonial Mexico* (Champaign: University of Illinois, Center for the Study of Reading, 1990).

52. See Michael Mallett and Christine Shaw, *The Italian Wars, 1494–1559* (New York: Routledge, 2012).

53. Book II, 69.

54. *Travels to Tana and Persia*, Book 1, 101.

55. Book I, 131.

56. Book II, 154.

57. Book I, 173.

58. Book II, 73.

59. Ibid., 99.

60. Ibid., 215.

61. Ibid., 69.

62. See Sylvia Wynter, "Unsettling the Coloniality of Being/Power/Truth/Freedom: Towards the Human, After Man, Its Overrepresentation—An Argument," *CR: The New Centennial Review* 3, no. 3 (2003): 257–337.

63. Margaret Small, "A World Seen through Another's Eyes: Hakluyt, Ramusio, and the Narratives of the Navigationi et Viaggi," in *Richard Hakluyt and the Travel Writing in Early Modern Europe*, ed. Daniel Carey and Claire Jowitt (Farnham, UK: Ashgate Publishing Company, 2012).

64. Richard Hakluyt, *The Principal Navigations* (New York: Penguin, 1972), 290–91.

65. Hakluyt, 292.

Chapter 4

Taking Action as the Damnés

> I have not the right to become mired by the determinations of the past. . . . The density of History determines none of my acts. I am my own foundation.
>
> —Frantz Fanon

> How many times have I been stopped in broad daylight by the police, who took me for an Arab, and when they discovered my origins, they hastily apologized; "Of course we know that a Martinican is quite different from an Arab." I always protested violently, but I was always told, "You don't know them."
>
> —Frantz Fanon

In this chapter I focus on people of color (POC) organizing as an intential project that foregrounds the human as a relationship and embraces the challenges of creating an ethical community across racial and gendered differences among the colonized. To call one together, such as in ethnic studies programs and queer people of color organizations, and so forth, there is an explicit project being hailed to forge active responses to the modern/colonial capitalist system, which includes critiquing the structural (economic, epidermal, social, and intersubjective) relations between individual members of different colonial/racial groups.

Chapters 1, 2, and 3 of this book all examined key themes shaping mixed race seriality: spontaneous racialized and gendered working class consciousness, visible race and lactification, and continental ontologies. Now we turn from examining the serial to the group. The two main terms I will be using here, "people of color" and "the damnés," do not supplant other self-identifying terms. Rather, they are identificatory terms that are in addition to other identities. Using "people of color" does not inherently demand abandoning one's history, community, or positionality. Rather, organizing as a person of color is necessarily situated and conditioned by one's particular experience and consciousness toward developing a collective. It is from a particular racial position that one engages the groups and because that process is ongoing, both the entanglements of identity and organizing are neither fixed nor determined. Kirstie Dotson and Elena Ruiz gave an apt warning of coming together across differences: these are not necessarily home spaces, rather they are the places where a particular kind of difficult work is conducted.[1] I do, however, challenge the notion that the term "people of color" is inherently or fundamentally antiblack or antithetical to indigenous sovereignty. I argue three main points for the continued efficacy of the term "people of color": that there is a politics of purity that undergirds some rejections of the term that needs to be challenged; there is an unacknowledged 250-year history of the term that has not been accounted for in critiques of continental ontologies; and that the relationship between language and the world is the construction of meaning and not pre-given.

A subtext to this argument is the premise that there is an important role for spaces that are specifically by and for people of color of all genders. There are many spaces for the coming together of colonial/racial subjects and white people toward social change that (ostensibly) should put the onus of reproductive labor on white peoples: LGBT centers, socialist organizations, most academic departments and related conferences, most non-profits, many night clubs, social gatherings, many community organizations, etc. On the other hand, people of color-specific organizations create an opportunity for intentional encounters between people of different colonial/racial groups to examine multistable oppressions, so that their embodied experiences (that are not reducible to each other yet do exist in relation to each other) can come to be seen and reflected on by larger collectives. They are necessary precisely because we cannot sufficiently account for the Manichean character of the colonial/racial condition from only one perspective.

EXAMINING OPPRESSION

A feature of any object of analysis, including intersubjective race, gender, and class relations, is that individuals can only see from where they are and are intending what they cannot directly see. A person of color organization can create the conditions for expanding perceptions through sharing experiences, critiques, and analyses from across multiple differences. The argument that relations between colonial-racial subjects are not possible is often premised on the erasure of Afro-indigenous peoples and other *castas* from the history of the Americas and the fact that many people are descendents of both African and Indigenous peoples, particularly in Spanish colonies. With the complex history of Afro-Latinxs in mind that is not reducible to, nor outside of visible race, we can talk about the need for an attitude of respect and a willingness to listen to the important asymmetries that threaten collaborative engagement as fundamental.[2] In fact, it is my argument that the building of this ethical community across colonial assymetries is the project of people of color spaces. The creation of spaces where grappling with the assymetries is possible are the concrete conditions in which a more robust decolonial feminist socialist theory can be developed. These encounters can unsettle presuppositions about oppression and force people to grapple with issues they might not understand as fundamental to their own positionality, provide opportunities to develop necessary communication skills to address them, and build theories and practices that do not fall into oversimplifications to facilitate the production of critical theories that are cognizant of the world as experienced by different colonial/racial groups. Specifically, the presupposition of some colonial/racial subjects that what happens to black people is not relevant to their own situation can be shown to be a profound misapprehension of the colonial condition.

It is important to underscore that these interactions are not happening on an equal playing field, and as such there are a few points that have been developed throughout this volume that are useful to reiterate here. First, the colonization of the Americas introduced a new kind of structural divide that is racial and continues to fundamentally shape the way that gender and class relations organize contemporary social relations. Second, the differences between colonial/racial subjects and between the colonized and the colonizers are not inherent or natural to the world, but rather situational and constructed. Third, people of color organizing is a specific type of organizing that colonial/racial subjects can choose or *not* choose to engage. If there is a preference for organizing within another type of group, people of color organizing does not displace that and we need not pretend it is an all or nothing dichotomy.

A central focus of this book has been to open up possibilities for being human other than those tied to the coloniality of being. Through a reexamination of eidetic memories and the semiotic structures that made particular experiences possible, a challenge that now emerges, after identifying the spontaneous form of oppositional consciousness that orients a mixed race woman of color of the damnés (chapter 1), exposing the Spanish colonial discourse of defining "mixed" people as new types in the hierarchy of Man produced as distinct from black, red, or white and thus key in the development of the politics of purity (chapter 2), and then identifying the semiotics of continental ontologies that negates the human and the relationships across these continents (chapter 3), is determining how the natally alienated mixed Latinx or Mexican woman needs to be responsive and responsible to this complex history in the fashioning of the self and the group. How in fact do we conceptualize the fashioning of the self?

I want to tease out two distinct definitions of history that I will use throughout this chapter to highlight some of the challenges that emerge from examining history as a colonized person. I want to bridge Fanon's call to distance ourselves from history with Linda Tuhiwai Smith's affirmation of "*re*writing and *re*righting" representations or exclusions from history. This effort is toward developing "a theory or approach which helps us to engage with, understand and then act upon history," and toward this end I will explain the key difference between these two definitions of history.[3] The second section of this chapter will unpack the existential challenges that "mixed" people can face in establishing a politicized collectivity based on a shared visibility through an examination of the contributions of philosopher Jennifer Lisa Vest. The struggle to be transparent, that is to appear as a racial, gendered, and classed solidity that can be clearly compared and reduced, reveals another path: a differential consciousness that affirms multiplicity as a political praxis of becoming and prioritizes creating an ethical community of the damnés. In fact, the struggle to be seen as a solidity, according to colonial logic, is indicative of the politics of purity that is the legacy of Spanish colonialism and it must be challenged.

The term *differential consciousness* is adapted from Chela Sandoval's definition: a form of oppositional consciousness that poetically transfigures and orchestrates "while demanding alienation, perversion, and reformation in both spectators and practitioners."[4] In other words, differential consciousness is oriented toward a notion of being that is in a constant motion of destroying and creating values and identities toward an ethical community. Differential consciousness segues with Sylvia Wynter's notion of *heretical* as the expression of a new subject position that permits functioning within, yet beyond, the demands of dominant ideology based on what is learned from a differential mode of consciousness. They both speak to embodied, historical, and fluid foundations for truth and value. Key to both Sandoval and Wynter's work is to demonstrate the ways in which the perspectives and worldviews of the damnés are excluded in fundamental ways even as they are selectively incorporated into colonial institutions. This insight on systematic exclusion/incorporation provides the acumen that there is a law-like pattern to these relations that follows not a pendulum, but the violent concentrations of capital into the hands of the white bourgeois ethnoclass. The related divisions that are produced between colonial/racial subjects through this pillaging of their bodies and lands is what people of color organizing can seek to examine and address.

Both Sandoval and Wynter underscore that the oppositional consciousness of different stratified groups of the damnés are not mutually exclusive. Rather, they note that the critical ways in which people have sought to redefine themselves away from dominant ideologies, for example from "negro" to "black," from "Mexican-American" to "Chicanx," from recalcitrant women to "U.S. Third World Feminists," have forced a reconceptualization of the human. It is the practice of forging "a redefinition of the relation between *concrete* individual[s] . . . and the socializing processes of the systems of symbolic representations" that this chapter is focused on as a path to collective action.[5]

HISTORY IN THE LIVED EXPERIENCE

There is a particular definition of history that Fanon is using when he states that "I am my own foundation" that is distinct from history as an academic discipline. Maurice Natanson offers this differentiation: history is concerned with the individuated manifestation of living reflectively in the midst of the social world seeking to transcend the limits of bad faith. History, on the other hand, is concerned with highly typified accounts of what happened in a certain period in the past.[6] He refers to them as microcosmic history and macrocosmic history, respectively. The focus of this chapter is at the crossroads of these two renderings of history: a microcosmic historical explication of the encounter with macrocosmic history as giving shape and coherence to one's future, including reflections upon which to orient future actions. The concern is that one of the practices of colonialism is to erase both the microcosmic and macrocosmic histories of the colonized, at the same time as weaving them out of a thousand fantasies, thus making macrocosmic history and theory from the perspectives of the colonized necessary decolonial efforts.[7] At the same time, foregrounding the first-person experience has not been presented in this book as a foundation of uncontestable evidence, but rather as a way to render everyday encounters to a methodological analysis. The terms in which one explains how the experience is made manifest among a field of other possibilities is a process of interpretation. This raises the question of the existential relationship between history and the futurity of the colonized.

To develop a practice that can better account for the reality of racialized existence and foreground the embodiment of consciousness in political praxis, I turn to the prose and poetry of an Afro-indigenous queer woman philosopher, Jennifer Lisa Vest. She states,

For I am more than my history
More than the symbol I seem
I am a soft skinned human being
And I have also cried myself to sleep . . .

Her statements can initially sound suspect as the call to place a distance between history and the self can appear questionable, given that the colonized are often cast as a people without history. However, the emphasis on the "distance" between one's history and futurity is probably one of the least understood positions in existential thought, yet one that is crucial for an analysis of a person's situation. It is a position that emphasizes the responsibility that one has for one's self that emerges from our very capacity as conscious beings. "I am more than my history" is a refusal of bad faith, but also a refutation of others who might continue to reduce her to the dehumanizing terms of colonial classifications. If Jennifer Lisa Vest says to us she is more than her history, than it forces us (even if for only a fleeting moment) to see ourselves as people who too might be more than our history. This pronouncement does not usher in another form of bad faith: that which asserts oneself as pure transcendence. Rather, Vest is seeking to articulate a closer connection between her embodied experience, the subjugated and intertwined histories of the Atlantic slave trade and settler colonialism, and political praxis that is negated under prevalent forms of organizing that demand solidity and an either/or positionality. To repeat after her, "I am more than my history," disturbs the perception that my facticity is a matter of fact, but rather something that I interpret and to which I constantly position myself in relation. Suddenly, transcendence is brought to the fore, escapable only through an act of negation or denial. Vest follows her statement on history with the assertion that she is a "soft-skinned human being," emphasizing a humanity above and beyond the overdetermined and overrepresented identity of being racialized/colonized, but yet embodied and visible to others. Vest's emphasis at this point on transcendence does not negate the structural conditions that constrain her possibilities. Rather, she begins the following sentence of the poem with crying: a necessarily social act of communication. The cry is fundamentally about a desire for recognition that denies her humanity; it calls for acknowledgment and expresses a hope to be comforted. The cry, found both in Fanon's and Vest's texts, is what precedes the words to explain one's course of action. It is a call to recognize the specific subjectivity of the individual, a subjectivity denied the colonized as living human beings.[8] Furthermore, it is a call to initiate a self/other dialogue for a cry desires to be heard. It is precisely the frustrated efforts of natally alienated Afro-indigenous mixed people to initiate a self/other dialogue between the damnés that is of concern here. The focus on this existential dilemma among the damnés is what motivates the re-evaluation of the search for belonging via two commonly sought approaches: the challenge that reading morphologies for evidence of kinship presents for "mixed" denatalized people, and the search for primary documents such as vital records as the litmus test of identity.

READING MORPHOLOGY AS COLLECTIVITY: CHALLENGES FOR AFRO-INDIGENOUS MIXED WOMEN

You look like my people, I tell her
Tracing the lines of my grandmothers
In the wrinkles around her eyes . . .

She laughs, doesn't answer
Asks
Who are your people?
That's a long and confusing story
I say . . .

We begin the investigation like a dance
With gentle probes
And speculations about blood
Geography, language, tradition

We take out paper, pens
Maps and photographs
Frantic for explanations
Search the shelves for snapshots
For the cousin, auntie
Ancestor who proves it
We sit close to touching
I trace my finger across her jaw
Try to grasp this resemblance . . .

In the end
Nothing exactly connects
We have, it seems, few traditions in common
No kin to call cousins
But I don't believe
I refuse to accept
These unwelcome answers
These concrete but false conclusions

I claim her anyway

—Jennifer Lisa Vest

At the beginning of this chapter I asked the question, How do we conceptualize the fashioning of the self? Vest's work offers rich opportunities for identifying key sites of a new poetics of reciprocal recognition. As mentioned earlier, Vest is of mixed African American and southeastern indigenous ancestry but is sometimes racially identified in different ways by others, depending on the context.[9] Furthermore, she identifies as a woman, but is sometimes read as a man.[10] Her appearing to others as different races and genders frame her face-to-face encounters and lived experience, shaping her subjectivity. Because of her "mixed" lineage as well as the ways others read her, for her to say "you look like my people" could mean she is speaking to any number of persons; black, Native American, Latinx, South Asian, mixed, man, woman, queer, and so forth. Vest begins with the practice of reading morphology as a way of identifying kin and draws the person in closer. The laughter of the other recognizes and acknowledges the effort to forge a familial bond, but there is also a discomfort, a distancing, and her desire to connect is met with a condition: "Who are your people?" The human is foregone as natal alienation is paradigmatic of the black, Afro-mixed, and Afro-casta experience, and detribalization is emblematic of colonial policies toward indigenous peoples. Despite an initial hesitancy shown by the other in the poem, a dialogue ensues between the two toward establishing terms for a familial bond. Evidence is sifted through and sought out, and again there is something in reading the contours of the face. Histories are narrated, stories are told, but in the end, there is no proof of filial kinship.

The last stanza of the poem unsettles the ways in which a people are determined and assessed. When read alongside Fanon's epigraph above, the insistence on forging a kinship connection is palpable. What is at stake is a struggle for existence itself in an antiblack colonial world. The desire to see the other as kin, as one's people, is also a call for the other to see her as kin, for a recognition of her humanity. In short, it is a call for a world of reciprocal recognitions, not between the damnés and the state, but between the damnés. How can this call for reciprocal recognition be manifest in a collective intention toward political action?

The call to organize as "women" has brought to the fore the fraught contradictions of gender in the colonial context. Vest has spoken in her work of the challenges her appearance presents to a dominant patriarchal society that reads human morphology not only in terms of visible race, but dimorphic types.[11] Reading morphology involves not only skin color and hair texture, but also the contours of the face and chest, skin texture, and hair distribution. What challenges does organizing on the terms of racialized gender present to people who are perceived as androgynous whether due to racial stereotypes or due to agential changes to their appearance, particularly when of the subproletariat? The racialized person's dilemma, including "mixed" people, is not a peripheral tangent from more central political issues, but rather one that is definitive of racial politics in the Americas. The hailing of certain people as "mixed race" or "racially androgynous" is in relation to others being hailed as not. Vest argues that "mixed" women face the curious dilemma of having no ontological resistance in the eyes of white people, but also not to many among the damnés—unless they can convincingly make claim to a singular racialized position (which is the focus of the work of many contemporary scholars hailed as "mixed").[12] The existential challenges that face the "mixed" person seeking to overcome bad faith raise fundamental questions about social ontology precisely because they are in relation to the possibilities and recognizability of action for all persons.

Michael Monahan has identified this conundrum as indicative of the politics of purity. He states, "Racial reality has been treated as something static. The politics of purity views racial categories as all-or-nothing sets of properties—necessary and sufficient conditions—such that any particular agent either is or is not a member of one and only one racial category. Given a phenomenological approach, however, race cannot be properly thought of as a matter of being but rather of constant becoming. . . . Thus, in asking what race is, we should *expect* ambiguity, contention, contestation, and even contradiction in the various responses worthy of consideration." However, in our current context, ambiguity, contention, contestation, contradiction, and change are rather seen as proof of falsehood, confusion, and/or illegitimacy. The assumption that a person must meet the necessary and sufficient conditions of either one race or another, is actually a legacy of Spanish colonialism. The person that experiences the world as "mixed race" is not the problem, but rather the problem is the coloniality of being that demands the politics of purity.

Specifically, it is Vest's recounting of an experience with police brutality that highlights not only how visible race, but gender, too, shapes encounters with state officials.[13] Being a racialized woman does not protect one from brutality in the way that being a white woman does. A consistent insight from women of color feminisms is that the experience of Black and Latinx peoples with the police demonstrates that there is a different semiotic structure of gender operating for colonial/racial subjects than for people racialized as white, particularly when signs of being working class are also involved. Quite literally, the dominant normative reading of the body as dimorphic types does not apply to the raced/classed body. Speaking to the issue of police violence as experienced across gender, race, and class differences, Andrea J. Ritchie offers this analysis: "Individuals perceived to be transgressing racialized gender norms or who are framed within gendered racial stereotypes are more frequently subjected to verbal abuse, invasive searches, and use of excessive force during encounters with police."[14] Note the tension in what she is saying: if one is perceived as a gendered racial stereotype, which likely involves class issues, then one is prone to experiencing police abuse. If one is transgressing gendered norms as a person of color then that, too, can lead to police abuse. In other words, Black and Latinx cisgendered women from the sub-proletariat, gender queer and trans women of color, and men of color across the gendered spectrum, are all subject to similar and increased forms of police brutality compared to those racialized as white. Incidents of state violence on the one hand and domestic violence on the other is one of the axes that propels organizing as women of color feminists: state violence negates dimorphism as a determinant category of social interaction and, conversely, domestic violence enforces dimorphism as a means of subordination and control. Coming to a feminist consciousness through these contradictory experiences of embodiment is necessarily going to come to radically different conclusions from white middle-class and bourgeois feminists. It is bringing into focus this reality that Maria Lugones' theory of women of color feminism works to do: intersectionality shows us what is missing when we separate race and gender from each other, but how do we conceptualize the very logic of the "intersection"? How do we think about the intersection so as to avoid separability? Lugones argues that gender is constituted by and constituting the coloniality of power.[15]

Seeking community through the reading of morphology involves not only race, but also sex-gender. Although both race and sex-gender are read morphologically (an overlap that lends itself to conflating the two), race and colonialism actually overdetermines gender. For an individual's gender identity to be recognized, the individual must be recognized as an other. The colonial/racial subject's subjectivity is, by definition, under erasure, and thus their gendered appearance, identity, and self-expression is overdetermined by racial (and sometimes classed) signifiers. For this reason, what it means to identify or be identified as a woman in a colonial/racial context means something distinct for the damnés.

In the above poem, Vest cites recognizability between the damnés as the necessary ground of legibility in a community or collective. We know that reading morphological differences can be a crucial way of identifying likely allies, shared experiences and histories, and defining the terms of a collective struggle. Conversely, reading morphologies as *naturalized* codes of difference has been instrumental in maintaining a stratified antiblack and misogynist world. Thus, reading across morphological differences is crucial for examining how differences are established, gaining a greater understanding of how that reading operates, how and in what way it constitutes subjects with particular points of view, and seeking ways to unsettle the naturalization of these codes. For the mixed woman of the sub-proletariat the relationship between recognizability and a particular point of view is a fraught one. What one knows about oneself is nowhere reflected in how one is seen. In this situation, the ideal scales upon which subjectivities are judged, compared, and accepted become the focus of the sub-proletariat, mixed race woman's attention. The mixed race damnés is confronted with several choices at this juncture, but one enticing choice is to look to archival research to determine and substantiate at least one part of an identity claim. One may anticipate the bad faith that is implicit to this choice, which we will examine now.

SEARCHING THE ARCHIVES FOR ROOTS AND BELONGING

Challenges for Natally Alienated People of Color

From a sense of determination to find a shared root and to forge a sense of belonging, Vest's poem speaks to the everyday practices through which we come to understand who "we" are in a modern/colonial context. Maps, photographs, and lists of people's names, places, clans, races, and tribes suddenly take on an interesting power to redefine a person's understanding of their positionality and connectedness in the world. If these documents are not readily available or they prove inconclusive, the individual might turn to state or church archives to seek more definitive evidence. In many cases, when individuals encounter legal classifications and documentation of a lineage that confirm or contradict their previous understandings of themselves, they then move out toward solidifying social relationships based on their newfound knowledge. Reinterpretations of socialization follow, efforts to reconnect with lost relatives are made, new friendship networks are forged, and new cultural orientations are taken. The evidence of history can compel a person to act differently, think differently, in short become different. It is precisely the force that vital records, primary documents, and macrocosmic historical information can have on a person that is under consideration here. For denatalized women of color who experience the world as morphologically stigmatized, but the struggle to find sufficient evidence of one's "roots" are frustrated or inconclusive as Vest discusses, there are two choices that appear: create a compelling claim to a *singular* racial identity through appeals to expand the normative definitions of the group (whether legal, morphological, or ideological) so as to be more inclusive whether on the basis of cultural tradition or politics, or turn toward asserting terms that emphasize multiplicity, ambiguity, or flexibility. *Mestiza*, *hapa*, and *creole* appear to affirm the latter, but they in fact tend to operate in practice like the former. However, there is a third choice that is possible even if less readily apparent, but it is politically salient and philosophically interesting: challenging the politics of purity.

The *Damnés* are Radical People of Color

Creating spaces where relations between concrete individuals of the damnés can be engaged, analyzed, and transformed is needed. Rather than an investment in roots and belonging for defining the terms of human sociality, the cry of the other asks that we take action against the logic and conditions that make the coloniality of being possible.[16] The decision to respond to the cry of the other does not emerge from a particular positionality or identity formation, but rather from a radical choice to embrace responsibility for the material, epistemic, and symbolic liberation of the dehumanized.[17] At the same time, positionality and identity are important terms on which political collectivities are forged as a means to navigate power relations between individuals, develop organizing skills among a particular group of people, as well as to articulate a shared position on a given issue. Under what terms can a call to organize be made that foregrounds the overcoming of bad faith, a common responsibility for the liberation of the dehumanized, a shared position on a given issue, as well as the need to navigate concrete interpersonal power relations informed by race, gender, and class?

In contrast to popular belief, the term "people of color" proves to have a rich transcolonial history stretching back three hundred years, as well as the important histories of coalition building under the rubric of "women of color" in North America.[18] As part of this effort, I want to connect organizing as "the damnés" with the history and practice of "people of color" as a way to further the decolonial project. First, I will examine two critiques of the term and then move on to expand on why the term still has important relevance for taking action.

Jared Sexton's critique of the term "people of color" has led some to a general skepticism toward using the term at all.[19] However, Sexton's critique is quite specific and is directed toward those who employ the term as a "refusal to admit to significant differences of structural position born of discrepant histories between blacks and their political allies, actual or potential." In other words, his critique is not a dismissal of the term generally, but rather when the term is deployed to evade the continued practices of antiblack racism. In fact, Sexton's critique is at a precise target, he states: "'people-of-color-blindness' . . . [is] to the precise extent that it misunderstands the specificity of anti-blackness and presumes or insists upon the monolithic character of victimization under white supremacy. . . ." Sexton does not propose to do away with the term "people of color," but rather to do away with the tendency to obscure the nadir position of antiblack racism in coloniality. Quite explicitly, he points to the important potential for a relational, rather than comparative, analysis within the term.[20]

Similar to Sexton, Debbie Reese critiques the term "people of color" in so far that it erases the specifics of settler colonialism and tribal nation's survivance. She wrote a brief essay titled "American Indians are not People of Color" that speaks to the growing skepticism of the term.[21] The essay raises several critical points for disentangling the particular struggles of sovereign tribal nations from the struggles of other subjugated peoples. She makes the crucial point that few people outside of tribal nations are even aware of the existence of tribal governments let alone the treaty or trust agreements that are still in effect. It is the invisibilization of indigenous struggles in many people of color projects that Reese writes against. Reese's argument against the flattening of the struggles of tribal nations into a people of color framework hinges on the assertion that what tribal people look like does not matter when it comes to issues of sovereignty, and thus whether one is "of color" or "not of color" (appearing white) is irrelevant. There is, however, an ongoing debate over this issue on how and to what degree antiblack racism impacts the terms of recognition *within* tribal nations and *between* tribal citizens, as Arica Coleman and Andrew Jolivette discuss regarding mixed Black-Indian people.[22] An examination of the term "people of color" in the history of the colonization of the Americas makes it apparent that it is precisely at the intersection of Black *and* Indian racialization that it was produced. In response to the skepticism toward the term "people of color," it appears that it was through efforts to natally alienate black and red peoples from the land and their relatives that the term was deployed. The following is a brief overview of the long history of "people of color" that complicates and expands the debates on the political saliency of the term.

The term "people of color" is said to begin in eighteenth-century French colonies as "gens de couleur libres," most often associated with freed people of "mixed" African lineage.[23] The assumption is that miscegenation was always between white and black, but the "mixing" involved indigenous peoples too.[24] In Haiti, the free people of color were the duplicitous mulattos that C. L. R. James described as those who vied to replace white colonists, but not coloniality.[25] However, even in Haiti the category of *affranchis* referred to both manumitted blacks as well as free people of color, and both were cast outside the definition of Man.[26] In the same time period, the term "gente de color" was used to refer to *castas* in places like Puerto Rico, Cuba, and Barbados.[27] In Mexico, *castas* were sometimes referred to as "gente de color quebrada."[28] Perhaps the most well-known example in the continental US of "people of color" was used in eighteenth- and nineteenth-century Louisiana to denote a class of Afro-mixed people who identified strongly with their "white blood."[29] But even there the category sometimes hid histories of resistance, including maroons who escaped to the city to pass as free people of color in addition to a more complex legal history of recategorizing Afro-indigenous peoples.[30] In the Eastern United States, "people of color" was also how American Indian, Black, *and* mixed Afro-indigenous people were sometimes collectively classified, as there was a tendency to record them as one group in Virginia's vital records.[31] The point here is not to give a comprehensive history of the term "people of color," but rather to demonstrate that it is a category that spans north and south, multiple colonialisms, and referred at different times and in different places to manumitted black peoples, indigenous peoples, *castas*, "mixed" people, and maroons. It has a complex history that provides the opportunity to think relationally and transnationally, all the while attentive to the specific histories of enslavement, colonialisms, manumission, survivance, and marronage. To speak to the specific situations of people named under the term "people of color" in different times and in different cultural regions demands situated, relational analyses that confront the relationship between structure and individual situations. Nowadays, in a US social justice organizing context, the term has been expanded to also refer to refugees and migrants from the global south. "People of color" in its current use is a political designation that, in its strongest examples, foregrounds a politics of solidarity. In an insightful commentary a person wrote, "I had to expand my identity in a way that tied me to Black people as part of their rebellion, not as the ringer that would suppress it. So I became a person of color."[32] It is precisely the historical and geographic breadth and complexity that the term "people of color" invokes that makes it a relevant term for decolonial organizing, not at the expense of more specific identities or groups, but rather as a clarion to all the damnés to gather for a purpose where a relational praxis will be foregrounded.

One of the challenges when organizing a community-based collectivity is choosing the terminology on which to make a call. It needs to convey the organization's unique purpose as well as communicate the ways in which the organization seeks to challenge a certain injustice. Sylvia Wynter has compellingly argued that asserting definitions of ourselves away from the "chaos roles" we have been ascribed in the current definition of Man enacts new ways of thinking of the human. It foregrounds how we know ourselves to be in the world and the roles that we have self-identified to enact. Rather than center the systemic subject, we instead focus on creating a new semiotic structure of self-representation as a way of invoking a new way of being in the world. It is with this in mind that I am proposing here a self-definition of *people of color* through the *damnés*.

Organizing as people of color of the damnés does not preclude identifying in more specific terms, but rather can be understood as an idiom to hail a relational politics where people of different racial/colonial experiences can know to gather to take responsibility for the liberation of those most dehumanized. Katherine McKittrick has termed this space as *demonic grounds*, a breaking of ground that acknowledges and strengthens the post-1492 culturally connective subject positions that make accepting flesh-and-blood humans as an interrelated, co-identified species.[33] As a matter of both microcosmic history and macrocosmic history, the term "people of color" can center an analysis of antiblack racism, colonialisms, border imperialism, misogyny, and heteronormativity in its analysis.

THE OPPOSITIONAL CONSCIOUSNESS OF THE DAMNÉS

When people of color of the damnés gather, demonic grounds cannot be *assumed*, they must be created and forged. The damnés will come from a variety of positionalities. Some will come to the group with a denouncement of antiblack racism, others with the conviction of indigenous sovereignty, others with an understanding of Mexican-hating, and so on. Often, and I think this is likely a crucial point, people will come to a people of color gathering with unique understandings that provide understudied insights, such as what it is to be black *and* Filipino, black *and* an immigrant, black *and* Latinx, and so forth. Gendered and working-class consciousness will vary too. The purpose of such a group is to come to a better understanding of how these different positionalities in the world relate to each other so that the full scope of how stratified capitalist societies are maintained and perpetuated can be better understood and changed. There are four priorities I want to highlight for organizing as the damnés: a relational analysis; differential consciousness; altericity; and the affirmation of multiplicity. These terms are likely unclear at this point, but they will be further explained below.

The relational analysis, as was described in chapter 3 and is here being developed as political praxis, is the approach to analyzing a particular racialized, gendered, and classed position in relation to other positionalities. Between the damnés, this approach emphasizes understanding that, for example, becoming black only gains its coherence in relationship to becoming indigenous and to becoming white, and so forth. Gender and class follows the same mode of analysis. A woman is not simply a category of nature, but a type of being that gains coherence in relation to men, nonbinary, and so on. A working-class person is in relation to not only the bourgeoisie, but also the sub-proletariat, and so forth. Implicit to understanding what role a given positionality has in the stratification of social relations is in and through the network of relationships that different positionalities have with each other. Rather than end an analysis with understanding how a particular racialized and gendered positionality functions in relation to only whiteness, men, or heteronormativity (i.e., Indian/white relations, the women/men binary, working class/bourgeoisie, etc.) the analysis continues with analyzing that function in relationship to other subjugated positionalities among and between the damnés, such as Indian/black relations, cisgender/trans of color relations, working class Latinx/middle-class Latinx, and so forth. The ways in which we delineate the differences between one positionality and another is an act of mediation and understanding how they are mediated is key to affecting change, both between individuals and at the structural level. It is my contention that we cannot fully know how differences are enacted between different positionalities among the damnés without direct interaction as critical thinkers speaking and working to establish an ethical community. As Jacqueline Martinez states, "The only way we come to create meaning and have experience is through relationships, and relationships of relationships." It is in and through the relationships between people of different positionalities that will make the pattern of an organizational fabric what it is.[34]

This particular mode of relational analysis is an enactment of differential consciousness. Differential consciousness is a mobile mode of consciousness first enacted by US Third World feminists that Chela Sandoval argued had the capability of aligning various worldwide social justice movements. Like US Third World feminist differential consciousness, the damnés' oppositional consciousness charts a topography of spontaneous consciousness that specifies the realities of specific experiences. Black, Mexican, Asian American, and tribally enrolled are four such examples. The damnés' oppositional consciousness delineates the pattern of critical points around which individuals and groups of colonial/racial subjects seek to transform the oppressive powers that shape their lives. These points are orientations that the damnés seek to redefine away from the terms enforced by the dominant social order, like Wynter's stated objective of creating new semiotic structures through which to define ourselves. However, rather than focus only on the relationship between the colonized and the colonizer, or between the working class and the bourgeoisie, the consciousness of the damnés in a person of color organization extends the analysis to *between* the damnés. In other words, the consciousness of the damnés does not assume a monolithic character of subjugation, but rather seeks to understand the particularities of different subject positions among the damnés and how their stratified relationship enables the modern/colonial/capitalist system. This kind of kinetic and self-conscious mobility of consciousness is utilized by the damnés to not only identify various colonial/racial/gendered subject positions, but the emergent forms of oppositional consciousness from those subject positions, and then develops a critical analysis that guides the enactment of ethical relationships based on these insights.

THE GIFTS OF THE DAMNÉS

The insights that the damnés have offered as gifts to the Eurocentric and white supremacist world would not only benefit the damnés, but all people.

However, Sandoval, Wynter, and Maldonado-Torres all note that the insights of the damnés are systematically negated in the modern/colonial world. In fact, Maldonado-Torres argues that this is the fundamental condition of the damnés: those who cannot give because things are taken from them. Generous reciprocity is impossible. Thus, a key struggle for the damnés is to create conditions in which they can give of themselves and have others be receptive of the expression of their loving subjectivities—basically an ordinary ethical community.[35] The vignette from the first chapter on the food program that created the conditions for a nascent ethical community is such an example.

Maldonado-Torres points out that when the loving subjectivity emerges, it is confronted by two camps: the slaves and the masters. When the damné faces another slave, rather than disavow her and turn toward the master to seek recognition there, the damné keeps looking to the slave and sees her as a relative. This is a radical move that changes the terms of recognition from the master to between slaves. The struggle for a world where the loving subjectivity of the slave can find its full expression necessarily lies in creating a world where the negation of reciprocity between slaves and masters is no more, but here I want to stay focused on developing relationships between the damnés that presupposes an account of the "mixed" colonial/racial subject. As many will note today, not all the damnés are or were slaves, and furthermore some were house slaves and others field slaves. Not all the damnés will look at their own situation and identify the same critical points around which individuals and groups can seek to transform the powers that oppress them. This is where the exchange of looks between the damnés can have difficulty manifesting as recognition. Despite their respective experiences of dehumanization (a negation of the self/other relationship), the differences can serve to replicate the *logics* of the master and slave. This is where listening to the voice of the other takes a central role so as to correctly identify various oppositional subject positions to then enact the terms for ethical relationships.

It is the decision involved in who to listen to that I want to underscore here. The dialectic between microcosmic history and macrocosmic history in the orientation of the individual must be motivated by *a decision* to be responsive and responsible to an other. It is the ethics of accepting the gift of insight and knowledge from those whose perspectives are rendered largely invisible, in this case, from other colonial/racial subjects, that affirms a particular sociality. This decision to turn to other colonial/racial subjects is not the result of external laws nor a dominant set of codes, but rather it emerges from the social constitution of subjectivity itself *and* a decision to be responsive and responsible to those rendered irrelevant in, for instance, dominant centers of knowledge production and decision making. This commitment to those who are seen as irrelevant or disposable involves frequent evaluations of who one is listening to in a colonial/antiblack world as power relations are not static and erasures are usually not apparent (hence they would not be *erasures*, *illegible*, or *invisibilized*). This is what can be called affirming opacity: to be open to the unknown, understand that the unknown is paradigmatic to what is known, and hold a commitment to be responsive and responsible to those seen as fundamentally invisible: disposable or irrelevant. In this way, the relationships that are forged form the texture of the weave of the organizational fabric.[36] Thus, the focus of organizing as people of color of the damnés is to explicitly incorporate the principle that our actions are the conditions on which new worlds are created, that our actions present us with new possibilities and reveal new obstacles. Neither can be known beforehand, and both are necessary for developing a political praxis. Rather than assert a static utopic vision, the utopia of the damnés will need revision and redirection depending on what the relationships reveal. It is in this sense that we can focus on weaving new individual and group perspectives into an organizational analysis and in terms of designing a pattern of ethical relations that strengthens and fosters a responsiveness to those most dehumanized.

THE ETHICS OF ORGANIZING AS THE DAMNÉS

What is the ethical relationship between the slave and the debt peon or between the house slave and the field slave in organizing to kill the master? Fanon offers this definition: organizing as the damnés is not premised on a sense of homogenous victimhood, nor from a collective identity that asserts a false equality between systemic differences, but rather from a loving subjectivity toward those "below." Fanon offers us an interesting perspective on the relationship between a damne's individual possibilities to affect change in a colonial antiblack world. He does not position himself as the always already slave, but as someone with a responsibility to respond to the cry of the other. This is quintessentially what he means when he states that he is his own foundation. The focus is away from his own "victimization" and toward the other to the point of substituting the demand to be recognized by the master for the work needed to establish reciprocal recognition between the damnés. Maldonado-Torres has named this ethical position *altericity*. As a model for organizers it goes something like this: I know the world through my embodied subjectivity, but my main responsibility is for the well-being of the other below. I look to the other below as my people. While my own experience of subjugation is what enlivens my spontaneous oppositional consciousness, I seek to overcome bad faith and transform the world not by only focusing on those with the same roots as me or those with a shared sense of belonging, and not only with those who are identified as the same systemic subjects, but I focus my efforts on the well-being of all those below and creating possibilities for the establishment of an ordinary ethical community. Organizing as the damnés, then, creates the conditions of possibility for developing a community that does not center on gaining recognition from masters or the state, but rather on creating recognition between colonial/racial subjects and developing an ethical community where the damnés can give of themselves and have their contributions received. As for the masters, they are forced to struggle for the recognition of the damnés in a context where the gifts of the damnés and the fostering of an ethical community among the damnés takes priority.

A question that haunts political organizers today is, Who exactly composes the damnés? The question of who is White, who is Indigenous, who is Asian, and who is Black preoccupies the current moment, with the endgame appearing to be whether a given group qualifies as an other to whom one is responsible. We can see the struggle to make sense of who "we" are as colonial/racial subjects in many efforts that are intent on creating a new world. The founding triadic schema of colonialism and slavery that structures contemporary social relations needs to be stretched by critical analysts to understand changing legal definitions of groups of people and changing demographics. As social contingencies change, colonial/racial/gendered subjects, including but not limited to the situation of new migrants, must learn about local histories so as to correctly decipher the conditions at hand. However, knowing everything about everyone is an impossible task, revealing the limits of using knowledge as the sole basis for forming collectivities. Furthermore, our facticities do not predetermine our orientations in the world, thus our actions cannot be predicted by referencing our histories as objects. We are, after all, conscious beings in relation with social structures. This insight puts us in a position of being attentive to not only that we are composites of social inequalities, but also that each person is a conscious individual with the capacity to judge the conditions at hand, take responsibility for their actions, take a stance, and join a collective struggle.

ON LANGUAGE

Now, there is a final point I want to make, and that is on the relationship between the world and language. The natural understanding of language assumes that words simply reflect a meaning that already exists in the world of objects. I find that, in some cases, the rejection of the term "people of color" relies on this understanding of language. However, the meaning of the world is constructed in and through language, which is not only situational but also one of the main tools we have to communicate. Participating in a people of color organization does not require that one accept a pre-given definition of the term, but rather actively engage to create what it means. As such, it is possible that one people of color group may in fact fail to see the specificity of antiblack racism as Sexton has stated, and another may make the analysis central. The point being, the politics of people of color organizing is not embedded in the nature of the term itself, but rather in the consciousness and actions of the members of the group. The history of the term invokes relations *between* black and indigenous peoples as well as the production of mixed Afro-indigenous people, so the term cannot be said to be implicitly ahistorical.

It is with these points in mind that I keep using the term people of color, particularly in certain organizing contexts. And I want to also bring to mind the orientations we see in texts like *This Bridge Called My Back*, Jacqui Alexander's *Pedagogies of Crossing*, Kristie Dotson and Elena Ruiz's work on coalitions and many others; that solidarity and coalition work have been central themes in the work of women of color feminist scholar/activists.

CONCLUSION

Racial identities mean more than only the oppressions we know them to entail. Black identity, Seminole identity, Chicana identity, and so forth, are likely important in ways that we can't foresee and additionally identifying as people of color can be a way to foreground the relational histories in which they are forged. To form a collective under the rubric of "the damnés" entails the ethics of a differential consciousness, a relational analysis, alterity, and the affirmation of the human as a relationship. It is impossible and undesirable to know absolutely everything about everyone, but we can know something about the coloniality of being and the way in which it stratifies people and negates self/other relationships. Naming ourselves from "people of color" to *people of color of the damnés* is to forge demonic grounds, foreground the relationship between different colonial/racial/gendered subject positions, redefine ourselves away from dominant definitions of Man, and usher in new terms for being human. It is the very choices we make regarding our symbolic self-representation in radical organizing that will in part guide our actions, as they are the decisions through which we actualize our mode of being as living, conscious, entities.

NOTES

1. Elena Ruiz and Kirstie Dotson, "On the Politics of Coalition," *Feminist Philosophy Quarterly* 3, no. 2 (2017): 13.

2. Ibid., 11.

3. Linda Tuhiwai Smith, *Decolonizing Methodologies: Research and Indigenous Peoples* (London: Zed Books, 1999), 29–36.

4. Chela Sandoval, "US Third World Feminism: The Theory and Method of Oppositional Consciousness in the Postmodern World," *Genders* 10 (Spring 1991): 3.

5. Sylvia Wynter, "1492: A New World View," in *Race, Discourse, and the Origin of the Americas*, ed. Vera Lawrence Hyatt and Rex Nettleford (Washington, DC: Smithsonian Institution Press, 1992), 47.

6. Maurice Alexander Natanson, *The Journeying Self: A Study in Philosophy and Social Role* (Reading, MA: Addison Wesley Publishing, 1970), 93–94. Note that Foucault's history sought to displace this distinction between microcosmic history and macrocosmic history. However, the specifics of responsible agency are never addressed by Foucault and still left for individuals to grapple with in the mundaneness of their individuated situations.

7. Smith, *Decolonizing Methodologies*, 1999; Fanon, *Black Skin, White Masks*, 2008.

8. Nelson Maldonado-Torres, *Against War: Views from the Underside of Modernity* (Durham, NC: Duke University Press, 2008), 133.

9. Jennifer Lisa Vest, "What Doesn't Kill You: Existential Luck, Postracial Racism, and the Subtle and Not So Subtle Ways the Academy Keeps Women of Color Out." *Seattle J. Soc. Just.* 12 (2013): 479.

10. Jennifer Lisa Vest, *Not Quite Right*, unpublished poem, 2012.

11. Vest, "What Doesn't Kill You," 482.

12. Jennifer Lisa Vest, "Being and Not Being, Knowing and Not Knowing: Mixedness Impossible," in *Philosophy and the Mixed Race Experience*, ed. Tina Fernandez Botts (Lanham, MD: Lexington Books, 2016).

13. Vest, "What Doesn't Kill You," 471.

14. Ed. Incite! Women of Color Against Violence, *Color of Violence: The Incite! Anthology* (Durham, NC: Duke University Press, 143).

15. Maria Lugones, "The Coloniality of Gender," *Worlds & Knowledges Otherwise* 2, no. 5 (2008): 4.

16. Nelson Maldonado-Torres, "The Topology of Being and the Geopolitics of Knowledge: Modernity, Empire, Coloniality 1." *City* 8, no. 1 (2004): 29–56.

17. Nelson Maldonado-Torres, "Post-Continental Philosophy: Its Definition, Contours, and Fundamental Sources." *Review of Contemporary Philosophy* 9 (2010): 4.

18. I use "people of color" rather than "women of color" here on out to be conscientious of gender fluid and non-gender binary identifying people. There is also a history to the term "people of color" that goes beyond the 1977 date offered by Loretta Ross for "women of color" in *The Origin of the Phrase "Women of Color"* or Fanon's use of "people of color" in *Black Skin, White Masks*. Furthermore, it is the strongest examples of people of color and women of color organizing and theorizing that I have in mind here. Strong examples of people of color theory and practice can be found in the work and writing of most of the writers I have been citing throughout this book. Alexander, *Pedagogies of Crossing*, 2005; Lorde, *Sister Outsider*, 2007; Sandoval, *Methodology of the Oppressed*, 2000.

19. J. Sexton, "People-of-Color-Blindness: Notes on the Afterlife of Slavery." *Social Text* 28, no. 2 (2010): 103.

20. Ibid., 47–48.

21. Debbie Reese, "American Indians are not People of Color," *ASCD Express,* Vol. 6, no. 15.

22. Arica L. Coleman, *That the Blood Stay Pure: African Americans, Native Americans, and the Predicament of Race and Identity in Virginia* (Bloomington: Indiana University Press, 2013); Andrew Jolivette, *Louisiana Creoles: Cultural Recovery and Mixed-Race Native American Identity* (Lanham, MD: Lexington Books, 2007).

23. William Safire, *Safire's Political Dictionary* (Oxford: Oxford University Press, 2008).

24. Andrew Jolivette, *Louisiana Creoles: Cultural Recovery and Mixed-Race Native American Identity* (Lanham, MD: Lexington Books, 2007).

25. C. L. R. James, *The Black Jacobins; Toussaint L'Ouverture and the San Domingo Revolution* (New York: Vintage Books, 1963), 163–73.

26. Roberts, *Freedom as Marronage*, 90, 97.

27. Kyzzy Sánchez Medina, *La esclavitud urbana en Santa Clara desde su fundación hasta 1797: hacia una interpretación contextualizada.* Trabajo de Diploma Universidad Central "Martha Abreu" de Las Villas Facultad de Humanidades Departamento de Literatura y Lingüistica, 2007–2008; Michele Reid-Vazquez, *The Year of the Lash: Free People of Color in Cuba and the Nineteenth-Century Atlantic World*, 2011; Jay Kinsbruner, *Not of Pure Blood: The Free People of Color and Racial Prejudice in Nineteenth-Century Puerto Rico*, 1996; Melanie J. Newton, *The Children of Africa in the Colonies: Free People of Color in Barbados in the Age of Emancipation*, 2008.

28. Soizic Croguennec, *Société minière et monde métis: Le centre-nord de la Nouvelle Espagne au XVIII Siécle* (Madrid: Casa de Velazquez, 2015), 262.

29. Alice Dunbar-Nelson, "People of Color in Louisiana: Part I," *The Journal of Negro History* Vol. 1, no. 4 (October 1916): 361–76.

30. Kimberley S. Hanger, "Patronage, Property, and Persistence: The Emergence of a Free Black Elite in Spanish New Orleans," in *Against the Odds: Free Blacks in the Slave Societies of the Americas*, edited by Jane G. Landers (New York: Routledge, 2013), 46. Andrew Jolivette, *Louisiana Creoles: Cultural Recovery and Mixed-Race Native American Identity* (Lanham, MD: Lexington Books, 2007).

31. Arica L. Coleman, *That the Blood Stay Pure: African Americans, Native Americans, and the Predicament of Race and Identity in Virginia* (Bloomington: Indiana University Press, 2013), xvi.

32. Rinku Sen, "Are Immigrants and Refugees People of Color?" *Colorlines*, July 10, 2007. Accessed July 27, 2016. http://www.colorlines.com/articles/are-immigrants-and-refugees-people-color.

33. McKittrick, *Demonic Grounds*, 136. For a recent example emerging from an ethnic studies department, see Evelyn Nakano-Glenn, "Settler Colonialism as Structure: A Framework for Comparative Studies of U.S. Race and Gender Formation." *Sociology of Race and Ethnicity* 1, no. 1 (2015): 54–74.

34. Jacqueline Martinez, *Communicative Sexualities: A Communicology of Sexual Experience* (Lanham, MD: Lexington Books, 2011).

35. Nelson Maldonado-Torres, *Against War: Views from the Underside of Modernity* (Durham, NC: Duke University Press, 2008), 153.

36. Edward Glissant, *Poetics of Relation* (Ann Arbor: University of Michigan Press, 1997), 189–190.

Conclusion

When Lewis Gordon published "Critical Mixed Race?" in 1995 the expression "mixed race" was apparently popular in academia.[1] It is slightly over twenty years later and the discussion of "mixed race" has been largely shunned in Ethnic Studies scholarship. Particularly after the 2008 publication of *Amalgamation Schemes*, it is almost impossible to speak of "mixedness" without immediate accusations of liberalism.[2] So then why speak of mixed race now?

"Can we keep the tacos and tamales, but get rid of the Mexicans?" jokes one person. "Can you please clean my table?" asks the fellow customer. "Build the wall!" chants the group. This book has focused on connecting the encounters experienced by descendants of working class *castas*—who are racially profiled, but are neither claimed by an indigenous community nor are visibly black—to a structural analysis toward developing a decolonial praxis. Here we are thinking about the appearance of the Mexican (as a racial stereotype that is extended to many Latinxs regardless of their specific histories) in the eyes of the US other, wherein the history of lynching, racial profiling, and mass incarceration has yet to be fully reckoned.[3] To provide some clear guideposts regarding what was covered in this book, I offer a point by point explanation of how this book differs from previous claims made by mixed race studies scholars. I reference the claims summarized in Gordon's work:

> 1. Accuracy and consistency of racial ideology demand a mixed-race standpoint, for if whites and blacks are "pure," then mixtures signify "other" forms of race. (This argument supports the reasoning behind constructing separate racial categories for mixed-race people.)

I do not argue that mixed people *are* another race or that a distinct mixed race standpoint is politically necessary but, rather, I theorize the construction of *casta* or "mixed race" as historically specific to the colonization of the

Americas. "Mixed races" have been constructed as "other races" as one of the means of social control in a context where the Spanish colonial elite were a small group with limited military capacity.[4] In this work I trace the construction of visible race through the colonial division of labor in Spanish colonies and argue for how it shaped embodied consciousness. Blackness, in this book, is defined as the negation of the self/other relationship and the institutionalization of dehumanizing practices. Although all colonized and enslaved peoples in the Americas were various shades of brown, some were designated as the visible *stereotype* of blackness, and this colonial legacy continues today. Unpacking this ontological shift while being cognizant that most organizing spaces and many Ethnic Studies scholars do not work within this understanding of blackness informs many of the moves I make in this book.

> 2. The question of accuracy raises questions of affiliation: filial recognition plays an important role in our self identities. The need to recognize one's ancestry fully calls for recognition of mixture. Saying that one's ancestry is all-black because of the "one drop rule," for instance, fails to identify relatives whose lineage is multiracial beyond their African ancestry.

History and filial affiliation are important, however the issue here is not entirely about accuracy. Rather, this book seeks to provide some insight on why it is that so many Latinxs are racially profiled, experience the second highest levels of incarceration and poverty in the United States, the lowest wages in California, and so forth, but no one can agree what visible race they (we) are. Some Latinxs may sometimes self-identify as white, but then admit no one sees them as such; they may identify as black, but then are told they are not; they may assert an Indigenous identity but then are told no community claims them. I argue that this is the conundrum created by the *sistema de castas* and the official color blind policies instituted in the nineteenth century by the elite in Mexico, that intersects with the racial discourse of the United States that is premised on the politics of purity.

> 3. On the biracial end, there is the fact of converging embodiments to consider: a biracial offspring "is" biologically and often culturally both of her or his parents.

In this book I explain that this way of thinking about human relations is itself a colonial construct. Surely there is another way of thinking about human relations across colonially instituted differences other than "racial mixing"?

> 4. If race means black or white, then mixture becomes an enigma. It signifies "racelessness." This argument goes both ways. In favour of a separate category

> for mixed-race people, it is advanced as a way of eliminating their exclusion from racial matrices by making such a provision. Against a category of mixed-race people, it is advanced to claim that even a racial designation will be an inaccurate articulation of their reality. And there are those who argue that it provides a critique of racial categories to begin with and perhaps point to a (raceless) future. These possibilities are discussed in Azck (1993, 1995).

I do not argue to make mixed race peoples separate categories, nor that asserting a mixed race category will lead to a raceless future. I do argue that an exposition of Spanish colonialism is necessary to understand the specifics of how Latinxs have been racialized. Castas were not raceless, rather they were constructed as other racial categories as a means of hegemonic social control. Rather than argue for the institutionalization of a mixed race category in the United States, I center a definition of the human as an embodied consciousness and a relationship as a way to counter the coloniality of being.

> 5. On the practical end, biraciality and mixed-race designations can serve as an anti-racist strategy: recognition of racial mixture dilutes identities premised upon conceptions of "purity" and can therefore be an important stage on the road to a raceless or more racially free future.

The Spanish colonial context already demonstrates that the recognition of racial "mixtures" does not dilute conceptions of racial purity, but rather upholds them. Rather than unsettle the logic of pure bloodedness, the notion of mixed blood only incited the desire for pure blood that remained steadfast even after independence in the regulation of intimacy between *güera*, *prieta*, *morena*, and so forth.

In this book, I do argue for the continued relevance of the term "people of color" as it is a term that is commonly used in organizing circles. Although "people of color" is often misconceived as a strictly contemporary term invented to address a problematically multiracial, multicultural, and/or mixed race group, I highlight the colonial history of the term that was borne from the redefinition of the human over the "long sixteenth century." I argue that it holds common-use potential for shifting the popular consciousness of the coloniality of being.

> 6. And finally, but not exhaustively, there is the existential claim: that mixed and biracial people have unique experiences that can be shared and cultivated through a recognized group identification. (This existential turn is also, of course, support for the political implications designated by (1).)

It is true that people perceived as "mixed" have unique experiences and may choose to write or organize on this theme, but a group identification with "mixed race" does not predetermine a particular politics nor preclude identifying with other groups. For example, an individual can belong to a people of color organization, a mixed race association, a Black professional group, and a Latinx one, and yet the politics of that individual cannot be assumed.

This book was written to contribute to a decolonial Latinx politics for and with a rapidly growing group in the United States who have had multiple studies written about them on their identity confusion, their internalization of racist and sexist norms, the frequent lack of correlation between their visible race and their identity, their criminality, as well as their social conservatism. Many of these studies treat Latinxs as a problem, rather than address the problems that Latinxs face. This book turns the tables and focuses on the challenges Latinxs face, namely the privation of history, a normative politics of purity, and a dominant definition of the human that renders colonial/racial subjects as less than deserving of a good life. One of the contributions that make this book unique is centering a definition of the human as a relationship, and thus developing a theory of affecting social change that is fundamentally about building relationships between colonial/racial subjects–the damnés.

I have centered the framework of *the damnés* so as to build and reaffirm the need for intellectual work specifically from working class people of color to address the structures of anti-black racism and settler colonialism, as well as build and affirm connections with social movements that are working towards creating a more humane world. This book makes an offering toward creating another world as an ongoing activity and practice of becoming.

NOTES

1. Lewis Gordon, "Critical Mixed Race?" *Social Identities* Vol. 1, no. 2 (1995): 381.
2. Jared Sexton, *Amalgamation Schemes: Antiblackness and the Critique of Multiracialism* (Minneapolis: University of Minnesota Press, 2008).
3. *Lynching in America: Confronting the Legacy of Racial Terror* (Montgomery: Equal Justice Initiative, 2015); Judith A. Greene et al., *Indefensible: A Decade of Mass Incarceration of Migrants Prosecuted for Crossing the Border* (Northampton: Grassroots Leadership, 2016); *Driving while Black or Brown* (Phoenix: ACLU of Arizona, 2008).
4. Ilona Katzew, *Casta Painting*.

Bibliography

Ahmed, Sara. "A Phenomenology of Whiteness." *Feminist Theory* 8, no. 2 (August 2007): 158.

———. *Queer Phenomenology: Orientations, Objects, Others*. Durham, NC: Duke University Press, 2006.

Alarcón, Norma. "In the Tracks of 'the' Native Woman." In *Between Woman and Nation: Nationalisms, Transnational Feminisms, and the State*, edited by Caren Kaplan, Norma Alarcón, and Minoo Moallem. Durham, NC: Duke University Press, 1999.

Alcoff, Linda Martin. "Sexed Identity as Embodied Horizon." In *Feminist Interventions in Ethics and Politics: Feminist Ethics and Social Theory*, edited by Barbara S. Andrew, Jean Clare Keller, and Lisa H. Schwartzman. Lanham, MD: Rowman & Littlefield Publishers, 2005.

———. *Visible Identities: Race, Gender, and The Self.* New York: Oxford University Press, 2006.

Alexander, M. Jacqui. *Pedagogies of Crossing: Meditations on Feminism, Sexual Politics, Memory, and the Sacred.* Durham, NC: Duke University Press, 2005.

Alliacus, Petrus. *Imago Mundi*. Boston: Massachusetts Historical Society, 1927.

Anzaldúa, Gloria. "La Prieta." In *This Bridge Called My Back: Writings by Radical Women of Color, Fourth Edition*, edited by Cherríe Moraga and Gloria Anzaldúa, 198–209. Albany: State University of New York Press, 2015.

Anzaldúa, Gloria, and AnaLouise Keating. *The Gloria Anzaldúa Reader*. Durham, NC: Duke University Press, 2009.

Apollodorus. *The Library of Greek Mythology*. New York: Oxford University Press, 1997.

Arens, William. *The Man-Eating Myth: Anthropology and Anthropophagy*. New York: Oxford University Press, 1979.

Aristotle. *Generation of Animals*. Translated by A. L. Peck. London: Loeb Classical Library, 1953.

de Beauvoir, Simone. *The Second Sex*. New York: Vintage Books, 1989.

Browne, E. G. *Arabian Medicine: The FitzPatrick Lectures Delivered at the College of Physicians in November 1919 and November 1920*. Cambridge: Cambridge University Press, 2011.

Byrne, Susan. *Ficino in Spain*. Toronto: University of Toronto Press, 2015.

Chanca, Diego Alvarez. "Second Voyage of Columbus." In *Select Documents Illustrating the Four Voyages of Columbus: Volume 1*. London: Hakluyt Society, 1930.

Charlesworth, Simon J. *A Phenomenology of Working-Class Experience*. Cambridge: Cambridge University Press, 2000.

Chevalier, François. *Land and Society in Colonial Mexico: The Great Hacienda*. Berkeley: University of California Press, 1963.

Cohen, Cathy J. "Punks, Bulldaggers, and Welfare Queens." *GLQ: A Journal of Lesbian and Gay Studies* 3, no. 4 (1997): 437–65.

Cohen, Simona. *Animals as Disguised Symbols in Renaissance Art*. Leiden: Brill, 2008.

Coleman, Arica L. *That the Blood Stay Pure: African Americans, Native Americans, and the Predicament of Race and Identity in Virginia*. Bloomington: Indiana University Press, 2013.

Columbus, Christopher. "First Voyage of Columbus." In *Select Documents Illustrating the Four Voyages of Columbus: Volume 1*. London: Hakluyt Society, 1930.

Cope, R. Douglas. *The Limits of Racial Domination: Plebeian Society in Colonial Mexico City, 1660–1720*. Madison: University of Wisconsin Press, 1995.

Croguennec, Soizic. *Société minière et monde métis: Le centre-nord de la Nouvelle Espagne au XVIII Siécle*. Madrid: Casa de Velazquez, 2015.

Crone, G. R., ed. *The Voyages of Cadamosto and Other Documents on Western Africa in the Second Half of the Fifteenth Century*. London: Printed for the Hakluyt Society, 1937.

Davis, Angela. *Blues Legacies and Black Feminism*. New York: Vintage Books, 1998.

de las Casas, Bartolomé. *Historia de las Indias*. Madrid: Impr. de M. Ginesta, 1875.

———. *Apologética Historia Sumaria, Volume 1*. Mexico: UNAM-Instituto de Investigaciones históricas, 1967.

Dotson, Kirstie, and Elena Ruiz. "On the Politics of Coalition." *Feminist Philosophy Quarterly* 3, no. 2 (2017): Art. 4.

Dunbar-Nelson, Alice. "People of Color in Louisiana: Part I." *The Journal of Negro History* 1, no. 4 (October 1916): 361–76.

Dussel, Enrique. *The Underside of Modernity: Apel, Ricoeur, Rorty, Taylor, and the Philosophy of Liberation*. Amherst, NY: Humanity Books, 1998.

"Dwayne's World." *Dwayne's World*, 2010. Accessed July 28, 2016. http://www.thescottishsun.co.uk/scotsol/homepage/sport/spl/3321720/Dwaynes-world.html.

Efferink, Leonhardt Van. "Martin Lewis: Metageographies, Postmodernism and Fallacy of Unit Comparability - Exploring Geopolitics." *Exploring Geopolitics*, 2015. Accessed July 27, 2016. http://www.exploringgeopolitics.org/Interview_Lewis_Martin_Metageographies_Postmodernism_Fallacy_Of_Unit_Comparability_Historical_Spatial_Ideological_Development_Constructs_Taxonomy_Ideas_Systems/.

Empedocles. *Empedocles: The Extant Fragments*. Edited by M. R. Wright. Cambridge: Bristol Classical Press, 1995.

Espiritu, Yen Le. *Body Counts: The Vietnam War and Militarized Refugees*. Oakland: University of California Press, 2014.

Fanon, Frantz. *A Dying Colonialism*. New York: Grove Press, 1967.

———. *Black Skin, White Masks*. New York: Grove Press, 2008.

———. *The Wretched of the Earth*. New York: Grove/Atlantic, Inc., 2007.

Febvre, Lucien, and Henri-Jean Martin. *The Coming of the Book: The Impact of Printing 1450–1800*. New York: Verso, 1997.

Forbes, Jack D. *Africans and Native Americans: The Language of Race and the Evolution of Red-Black Peoples*. Champaign: University of Illinois Press, 1993.

Forman, Murray. *The 'Hood Comes First: Race, Space, and Place in Rap and Hip-Hop*. Middletown, CT: Wesleyan University Press, 2002.

Foucault, Michel. *The Order of Things: An Archaeology of the Human Sciences*. New York: Vintage Books, 1970.

Galen. *On Semen*. Translated by Phillip De Lacy. Berlin: Akademie Verlag GmbH, 1992.

———. *On The Elements According to Hippocrates*. Translated by Phillip De Lacy. Berlin: Akademie Verlag GmbH, 1996.

Galsco, Sharon Bailey. *Constructing Mexico City: Colonial Conflicts over Culture, Space, and Authority*. New York: Palgrave Macmillan, 2010.

Global News. "Public Housing Residents Face Stereotypes, Stigma That Burdens Community." July 17, 2012. Accessed July 28, 2016. http://globalnews.ca/news/267249/public-housing-residents-face-stereotypes-stigma-that-burdens-community/.

Goldenberg, David M. *The Curse of Ham: Race and Slavery in Early Judaism, Christianity, and Islam*. Princeton, NJ: Princeton University Press, 2003.

Gonzalez, Francisco J. "Of Beasts and Heroes: The Promiscuity of Humans and Animals in the Myth of Er." In *Plato's Animals: Gadflies, Horses, Swans, and Other Philosophical Beasts*, edited by Jeremy Bell and Michael Naas, 225–45. Bloomington: Indiana University Press, 2015.

Gordon, Lewis R. "Race, Theodicy, and the Normative Emancipatory Challenges of Blackness." *South Atlantic Quarterly* 112, no. 4 (2013): 725–36.

———. *His Majesty's Other Children: Sketches of Racism from a Neocolonial Age*. Lanham, MD: Rowman & Littlefield Publishers, 1997.

———. "Critical Mixed Race?" *Social Identities* 1, no. 2 (1995).

———. *Bad Faith and Antiblack Racism*. Amherst, NY: Humanity Press, 1995.

———. *Existentia Africana: Understanding Africana Existential Thought*. New York: Routledge, 2000.

———. *Fanon and the Crisis of European Man: An Essay on Philosophy and the Human Sciences*. New York: Routledge, 1995.

Greenblatt, Stephen. *Renaissance Self-Fashioning: From More to Shakespeare*. Chicago: The University of Chicago Press, 2005.

Hanger, Kimberly S. "Patronage, Property, and Persistence: The Emergence of a Free Black Elite in Spanish New Orleans." In *Against the Odds: Free Blacks in the Slave Societies of the Americas*, edited by Jane G. Landers. New York: Routledge, 2013.

Hanke, Lewis. *Bartolomé de Las Casas: Bookman, Scholar and Propagandist*. Philadelphia: University of Philadelphia Press, 1952.

Hayer, Teresa. *The Creation of World Poverty: An Alternative View to the Brandt Report*. London: Pluto Press, 1987.

Hayes, Cressida. "Changing Race, Changing Sex: The Ethics of Self-Transformation." *Journal of Social Philosophy* 2, no. 37 (Summer 2006): 266–82.

Hegel, Georg Wilhelm Friedrich, and J. Sibree. *The Philosophy of History*. New York: Dover Publications, 1956.

Heidegger, Martin. *Being and Time*. New York: Harper, 1962.

Hernandez-Avila, Ines. "Relocations upon Relocations: Home, Language, and Native American Women's Writings." *American Indian Quarterly* 19, no. 4 (1995): 491–507.

Hilliard, David, and The Dr. Huey P. Newton Foundation. *The Black Panther Party Service to the People Programs*. Albuquerque: University of New Mexico Press, 2010.

Hodgen, Margaret T. *Early Anthropology in the Sixteenth and Seventeenth Centuries*. Philadelphia: University of Pennsylvania Press, 1964.

Hodgson, Marshall. *The Venture of Islam Vol. 1, 2 and 3*. Chicago: The University of Chicago Press, 1977.

hooks, bell. *Where We Stand: Class Matters*. New York: Routledge, 2000.

Husserl, Edmund. *The Crisis of European Sciences and Transcendental Phenomenology: An Introduction to Phenomenological Philosophy*. Evanston, IL: Northwestern University Press, 1970.

Imber, Colin. *The Ottoman Empire, 1300–1650: The Structure of Power*. New York: Palgrave Macmillan, 2002.

Ivins Jr., William M. *Prints and Visual Communication*. Cambridge, MA: Harvard University Press, 1953.

James, C. L. R. *The Black Jacobins; Toussaint L'Ouverture and the San Domingo Revolution*. New York: Vintage Books, 1963.

Janani. "What's Wrong With the Term 'Person of Color.'" *Black Girl Dangerous*, March 20, 2013. Accessed July 27, 2016. http://www.blackgirldangerous.org/2013/03/2013321whats-wrong-with-the-term-person-of-color/.

Jiménez, Robert T. *The History of Reading and the Uses of Literacy in Colonial Mexico*. Champaign: University of Illinois, Center for the Study of Reading, 1990.

Jolivette, Andrew. *Louisiana Creoles: Cultural Recovery and Mixed-Race Native American Identity*. Lanham, MD: Lexington Books, 2007.

Karras, Ruth Mazo. *Sexuality in Medieval Europe*. London: Routledge, 2012.

Katzew, Ilona. *Casta Painting: Images of Race in Eighteenth-century Mexico*. New Haven, CT: Yale University Press, 2005.

Kelley, Robin D. G. *Race Rebels: Culture, Politics, and the Black Working Class*. New York: Free Press, 1994.

Kellogg, Susan. "From Parallel and Equivalent to Separate but Unequal: Tenochca Mexica Women, 1500–1700." *Indian Women of Early Mexico* (1997): 123–43.

Kim, Susan M. "Man-Eating Monsters and Ants as Big as Dogs." In *Animals and the Symbolic in Mediaeval Art and Literature*, edited by L. A. J. R. Houwen. Groningen, NL: Egbert Forsten, 1997.

Kinsbruner, Jay. *Not of Pure Blood: The Free People of Color and Racial Prejudice in Nineteenth-Century Puerto Rico*. Durham, NC: Duke University Press, 1996.

Konrad, Herman W. *A Jesuit Hacienda in Colonial Mexico: Santa Lucía, 1576–1767*. Palo Alto, CA: Stanford University Press, 1980.

Kozloff, Nikolas. "A Real Racial Democracy? Hugo Chávez and the Politics of Race." *Counterpunch*, October 14, 2005. http://www.counterpunch.org/2005/10/14/hugo-ch-aacute-vez-and-the-politics-of-race/.

Kretzmann, Norman, Anthony Kenny, and Jan Pinborg, eds. *The Cambridge History of Later Medieval Philosophy: From the Rediscovery of Aristotle to the Disintegration of Scholasticism, 1100–1600*. Cambridge, MA: Cambridge University Press, 1988.

Kruks, Sonia. "Identity Politics and Dialectical Reason: Beyond an Epistemology of Provenance." *Hypatia* 10, no. 2 (Spring 1995): 1–22.

Kyzzy Sánchez Medina. *La esclavitud urbana en Santa Clara desde su fundación hasta 1797: hacia una interpretación contextualizada*. Trabajo de Diploma Universidad Central "Martha Abreu" de Las Villas Facultad de Humanidades Departamento de Literatura y Lingüistica, 2007–2008.

Lestringant, Frank. *Cannibals: The Discovery and Representation of the Cannibal from Columbus to Jules Verne*. Berkeley: University of California Press, 1997.

Lewis, Martin W., and Karen Wigen. *The Myth of Continents: A Critique of Metageography*. Berkeley: University of California Press, 1997.

Linebaugh, Peter, and Marcus Redicker. *The Many-Headed Hydra: The Hidden History of the Revolutionary Atlantic*. Boston: Beacon Press, 2001.

Lowe, Kate. "Introduction: The Black African Presence in Renaissance Europe." In *Black Africans in Renaissance Europe*, edited by T. F. Earle and K. J. P. Lowe, 1–16. Cambridge: Cambridge University Press, 2010.

Lowe, Lisa. "The Intimacies of Four Continents." In *Haunted by Empire: Geographies of Intimacy in North American History*. Durham, NC: Duke University Press, 2006.

Lughod, Janet Abu. *Before European Hegemony: The World System A.D. 1250–1350*. New York: Oxford University Press, 1989.

Lugones, Maria. "Heterosexualism and the Colonial / Modern Gender System." *Hypatia* 22, no. 1 (2007): 186–219.

———. "The Coloniality of Gender." *Worlds & Knowledges Otherwise* 2, no. 5 (2008): 1–17.

MacNutt, Francis Augustus. *De Orbe Novo: The Right Decades of Peter Martyr D'Anghera*. New York: G. P. Putnam's Sons, 1912.

Mahonty, Chandra Talpade. *Feminism without Borders*. Durham, NC: Duke University Press, 2003.

Maldonado-Torres, Nelson. "The Topology of Being and the Geopolitics of Knowledge: Modernity, Empire, Coloniality 1." *City* 8, no. 1 (2004): 29–56.

———. *Against War: Views from the Underside of Modernity*. Durham, NC: Duke University Press, 2008.

———. "Post-Continental Philosophy: Its Definition, Contours, and Fundamental Sources." *Review of Contemporary Philosophy* 9 (2010): 40.

———. "Thinking through the Decolonial Turn: Post-Continental Interventions in Theory, Philosophy, and Critique—An Introduction." *Transmodernity: Journal of Peripheral Cultural Production of the Luso-Hispanic World* 1, no. 2 (2011).

Martínez, María Elena. *Genealogical Fictions: Limpieza de Sangre, Religion, and Gender in Colonial Mexico*. Palo Alto, CA: Stanford University Press, 2008.

Martinez, Jacqueline M. *Phenomenology of Chicana Experience and Identity: Communication and Transformation in Praxis*. Lanham, MD: Rowman & Littlefield, 2000.

Marx, Karl. *Economic and Philosophic Manuscripts of 1844*. Amherst, NY: Prometheus Books, 1988.

Marx, Karl, and Friedrich Engels. *The Communist Manifesto*. New York: International Publishers Co., 2014.

Marx, Karl, and Friedrich Engels. *German Ideology*. Amherst, NY: Prometheus Books, 1998.

Mbembe, Achille. "Necropolitics." *Public Culture*. 15, no. 1 (Winter 2003).

McClintock, Anne. *Imperial Leather: Race, Gender and Sexuality in the Colonial Conquest*. New York: Routledge, 1995.

McKittrick, Katherine. *Demonic Grounds: Black Women and the Cartographies of Struggle*. Minneapolis: University of Minnesota Press, 2006.

Mela, Pomponius. *De situ orbis, libri tres*. Salamanca: Diego Cussío, 1598.

Mills, Kenneth B., William B. Taylor, and Sandra Lauderdale Graham, eds. *Colonial Latin America: A Documentary History*. Lanham, MD: Rowman & Littlefield, 2002.

Minh-ha, Trinh T. *Woman, Native, Other: Writing Postcoloniality and Feminism*. Bloomington: Indiana University Press, 1989.

Monahan, Michael. *The Creolizing Subject*. New York: Fordham University Press, 2011.

Montalboddo, Fracanzano da. *Paesi Nouamente Retrovati & Novo Mondo da Alberico Vesputio Florentino Intitulato*. Princeton, NJ: Princeton University Press, 1916.

Moraga, Cherríe. "La Güera." In *This Bridge Called My Back: Writings by Radical Women of Color, Fourth Edition*, edited by Cherríe Moraga and Gloria Anzaldúa. Albany: State University of New York Press, 2015.

Mörner, Magnus. *Race Mixture in the History of Latin America*. Boston: Little, Brown, 1967.

Moyssén, Xavier. "La primera academia de pintura en Mexico." *Anales del Instituto de Investigaciones Esteticas, UNAM* IX, no. 34 (1965): 15–30.

Mudimbe, V. Y. *The Idea of Africa: Gnosis, Philosophy, and the Order of Knowledge*. Bloomington: Indiana University Press, 1994.

Natanson, Maurice Alexander. *The Journeying Self: A Study in Philosophy and Social Role*. Boston: Addison-Wesley Educational Publishers Inc., 1970.

Newton, Melanie J. *The Children of Africa in the Colonies: Free People of Color in Barbados in the Age of Emancipation*. Baton Rouge: Louisiana State University Press, 2008.

Nunn, George. "The Imago Mundi and Columbus." *The American Historical Review* 40, no. 4 (1935): 646–61.

O'Crowley, Pedro Alonso. *A Description of the Kingdom of New Spain*. Translated and edited by Sean Galvin. San Francisco: John Howell Books, 1972.

Oliver, Kelly. *The Colonization of Psychic Space: A Psychoanalytic Social Theory of Oppression*. Minneapolis: University of Minnesota Press, 2004.

Omi, Michael, and Howard Winant. *Racial Formation in the United States: From the 1960s to the 1990s*. New York: Routledge, 1994.

Overall, Christine. "Nowhere at Home: Toward a Phenomenology of Class Consciousness." In *This Fine Place So Far from Home: Voices of Academics from the Working Class*, edited by Carlos L. Dews, 209–20. Philadelphia: Temple University Press, 1995.

Pagden, Anthony. *The Fall of Natural Man: The American Indian and the Origins of Comparative Ethnology*. Cambridge, MA: Cambridge University Press, 1982.

Patterson, Orlando. *Slavery and Social Death: A Comparative Study*. Cambridge, MA: Harvard University Press, 1982.

Plato. "Phaedrus." In *Plato Complete Works*, edited by John M. Cooper, 506–56. Indianapolis: Hackett Publishing Company, Inc., 1997.

———. "Statesman." In *Plato Complete Works*, edited by John M. Cooper, 294–358. Indianapolis: Hackett Publishing Company, Inc., 1997.

Pliny the Elder. *Pliny's Natural History: A Selection from Philemon Holland's Translation*. Edited by J. Newsome. Oxford: Clarendon Press, 1964.

Ponty, Maurice M. *Phenomenology of Perception*. London: Routledge, 2002.

Ramusio, Giovanni Battista. *Delle Navigazioni e Viaggi*. Torino: G. Einaudi, 1978.

Randles, W. G. L. "Classical Models of World Geography and Their Transformation Following the Discovery of America." In *The Classical Tradition and the Americas*, edited by Wolfgang Haase and Meyer Reinhold, 5–76. New York: Walter de Gruyter & Co., 1993.

Reed, Adolph. *The Underclass as Myth and Symbol: The Poverty of Discourse about Poverty*. Alternative Education Project, 1992.

Reese, Debbie. "American Indians are not People of Color." *ASCD Express* 6, no. 15.

Reid-Vazquez, Michele. *The Year of the Lash: Free People of Color in Cuba and the Nineteenth-Century Atlantic World*. Athens: University of Georgia Press, 2011.

Roberts, Neil. *Freedom as Marronage*. Chicago: The University of Chicago Press, 2015.

Rose, Tricia. *Black Noise: Rap Music and Black Culture in Contemporary America*. Hanover, NH: University Press of New England, 1994.

Safire, William. *Safire's Political Dictionary*. Oxford: Oxford University Press, 2008.

Sandoval, Chela. *Methodology of the Oppressed*. Minneapolis: University of Minnesota Press, 2000.

Sartre, Jean-Paul. *Being and Nothingness*. New York: Open Road Media, 2012.

———. *Being and Nothingness*. New York: Washington Square Press, 1993.

———. *Critique of Dialectical Reason, Volume One*. New York: Verso, 1960.

Seed, Patricia. "Social Dimensions of Race: Mexico City, 1753." *The Hispanic American Historical Review* 62 (1982): 569–606.

———. *To Love, Honor, and Obey in Colonial Mexico: Conflicts over Marriage Choice, 1574–1821*. Palo Alto, CA: Stanford University Press, 1988.

———. *American Pentimento: The Invention of Indians and the Pursuit of Riches*. Minneapolis: University of Minnesota Press, 2001.

Sekyi-Otu, Ato. *Fanon's Dialectic of Experience*. Cambridge, MA: Harvard University Press, 1996.

Sen, Rinku. "Are Immigrants and Refugees People of Color?" *Colorlines*, July 10, 2007. Accessed July 27, 2016. http://www.colorlines.com/articles/are-immigrants-and-refugees-people-color.

Sexton, Jared. *Amalgamation Schemes: Antiblackness and the Critique of Multiracialism*. Minnesota: University of Minnesota Press, 2008.

———. "People-of-Color-Blindness: Notes on the Afterlife of Slavery." *Social Text* 28, no. 2 (2010): 31–56.

Smith, Linda Tuhiwai. *Decolonizing Methodologies: Research and Indigenous Peoples*. London: Zed Books, 1999.

Sokolowski, Robert. *Husserlian Meditations: How Words Present Things*. Evanston, IL: Northwestern University Press, 1974.

Suarez-Krabbe, Julia. *Race, Rights, Rebels: Alternatives to Human Rights and Development from the Global South*. Lanham, MD: Rowman & Littlefield International, 2016.

Tang, Eric. *Unsettled: Cambodian Refugees in the New York City Hyperghetto*. Philadelphia: Temple University Press, 2015.

Taylor-Garcia, Daphne V. "The Discursive Construction of 'Women' in Las Americas: An Analysis of Sixteenth-Century Print Culture." *Decolonizing the Digital/Digital Decolonization (II)* 3, no. 1 (2009). Accessed March 23, 2016. https://globalstudies.trinity.duke.edu/volume-3-dossier-1-decolonizing-the-digitaldigital-decolonization-p-2.

———. "Decolonial Historiography: Thinking about Land and Race in a Transcolonial Context." *InTensions Journal* 6 (Fall/Winter 2012).

Tovar de Teresa, Guillermo. *Miguel Cabrera: Drawing Room Painter of the Heavenly Queen*. Mexico: InverMexico Grupo Financiero, 1995.

Tyrrell, William Blake. *Amazons: A Study in Athenian Mythmaking*. Baltimore: Johns Hopkins University Press, 1984.

Vest, Jennifer Lisa. "The Promise of Caribbean Philosophy: How It Can Contribute to a 'New Dialogic' in Philosophy." *Caribbean Studies* 33, no. 2 (2005): 3–34.

———. "The Internally Globalized Body as Instigator: Crossing Borders, Crossing Races." In *Florida without Borders: Women at the Intersections of the Local and Global*, edited by Sharon Hayden, Kay Masters, Judy A., and Kim Vaz. Newcastle: Cambridge Scholars Publishing, 2008.

———. "What Doesn't Kill You: Existential Luck, Postracial Racism, and the Subtle and Not So Subtle Ways the Academy Keeps Women of Color Out." *Seattle J. Soc. Just.* 12 (2013): 471–518.

———. *'You Look Like My People' Jennifer Lisa Vest: Mixed Race Artist, Author, and Lecturer*. Accessed July 28, 2016. http://www.jenniferlisavest.com/#!videos.

———. "Being and Not Being, Knowing and Not Knowing." In *Philosophy and the Mixed Race Experience*, edited by Tina Fernandes-Botts et al. London: Lexington Books, 2016.

Vidal-Ortiz, Salvador. "People of Color." Edited by Richard T. Schaefer. *Encyclopedia of Race, Ethnicity, and Society* 1 (2008).

Vinson III, Ben. “Moriscos y lobos en Nueva Espana.” In *Debates Historicos contemporaneos: Africanos y Afrodescendientes en Mexico y Centroamérica*, edited by María Elisa Velásquez, 159–78. Mexico DF: Centro de Estudios de Mexicanos y Centroamericanos, 2011.

Wacquant, Loïc J. D. *Urban Outcasts: A Comparative Sociology of Advanced Marginality*. Cambridge: Polity Press, 2008.

Walia, Harsha. *Undoing Border Imperialism*. Oakland, CA: AK Press, 2013.

Walker, Alice. *In Search of Our Mothers' Gardens: Womanist Prose*. New York: Mariner Books, 2003.

Wilderson III, Frank B. *Red, White, and Black: Cinema and the Structure of U.S. Antagonisms*. Durham, NC: Duke University Press, 2010.

Worsley, Peter. “Frantz Fanon and the ‘Lumpenproletariat.’” *The Socialist Register* 9 (1972).

Wynter, Sylvia. “1492: A New World View.” In *Race, Discourse, and the Origin of the Americas: A New World View*, edited by Vera Lawrence Hyatt and Rex Nettleford. Washington, DC: Smithsonian Institution Press, 1995.

———. “Beyond Miranda's Meaning: Un/Silencing the ‘Demonic Ground’ of Caliban's ‘Woman.’” In *Out of Kumbla: Caribbean Women and Literature*, edited by Carole Boyce Davies and Elaine Savory Fido, 355–66. Trenton, NJ: African World Press, 1990.

———. “On How We Mistook the Map for the Territory, and Reimprisoned Ourselves in Our Unbearable Wrongness of Being, of Desêtre: Black Studies Toward the Human Project.” In *A Companion to African-American Studies*, edited by Lewis R. Gordon and Jane Anna Gordon, 107–118. Malden, MA: Blackwell Publishing, 2006.

———. “The Ceremony Must Be Found: After Humanism.” *Boundary 2* 12, no. 3 (1984): 19–70.

———. “Unsettling the Coloniality of Being/Power/Truth/Freedom: Towards the Human, After Man, Its Overrepresentation—An Argument.” *CR: The New Centennial Review* 3, no. 3 (2003): 257–337.

X, Malcolm, and Alex Haley. *The Autobiography of Malcolm X*. New York: Ballantine Books, 1992.

Yancey, George A. *Who Is White? Latinos, Asians, and the New Black/Nonblack Divide*. Boulder, CO: L. Rienner, 2003.

Young, Iris Marion. “Gender as Seriality: Thinking about Women as a Social Collective.” *Signs* 19, no. 3 (Spring 1994): 713–38.

Zack, Naomi. *Race and Mixed Race*. Philadelphia: Temple University Press, 1993.

Index

About the Author

Daphne V. Taylor-García is assistant professor of ethnic studies at the University of California, San Diego.

Lightning Source UK Ltd.
Milton Keynes UK
UKHW01n1541120618
324130UK00001B/8/P